M000190102

LOST
LESSONS

By

Dr. Randy T. Johnson
and
David Rutledge

ZOË LIFE
PUBLISHING
WORDS to LIVE BY

Published by:
Zoe Life Publishing
P.O. Box 871066
Canton, MI 48187 USA
www.zoelifepub.com

All Scripture quotations, unless otherwise indicated, are taken from Holy Bible, New International Version NIV ® copyright © 1973, 1978, 1984 by International Bible Society.

Take note that the name satan and associated names are not capitalized. We choose not to give him any preeminence, even to the point of violating grammatical rules.

Author: Dr. Randy T. Johnson, David Rutledge
Cover Design: David Rutledge

First U.S. Edition Year 1st Edition was Published

Publisher's Cataloging-In-Publication Data

Johnson, Randy and Rutledge, David

Lost Lessons
Summary: Christian devotional based on the television series Lost (r).

13 Digit ISBN 978-1-934363-80-5

1.Christian Living, Spiritual Growth, Lost, Christianity, Religion

For current information about releases by Dr. Randy T. Johnson or David Rutledge or other releases from Zoe Life Publishing, visit our web site: http://www.zoelifepub.com

Printed in the United States of America

v3 02 23 2011

Acknowledgements

To the *I AM*, may you use this simple offering in spite of itself. To my parents, for a lifetime of love, encouragement, and showing me a life spent serving Christ. To Doc, from the thousands of kids that you have inspired, and from this kid, who you continue to inspire; thanks for the years of example and all your hard work on this project! To my favorite person, for your heart, your love, and the truth.

—Dave

Dedicate to my wife, with much gratitude to my children and parents. Thank you Lord for fresh opportunities to serve.

—Randy

We both want to thank Ann Klein for her insight and direction on this book.

LOST
LESSONS

By

Dr. Randy T. Johnson
and
David Rutledge

Contents

How to use this Book

LOST Lessons was created to be used in two **ways.** First, this book can be used as a personal devotion. Simply go through the devotions, read the scriptures and answer the questions. Allow God to open your heart to the message He has for you, let His desires change your spirit, mind, and actions. Use the questions to help apply the biblical truths to your life, the scriptures in the further study section to dig deeper, and the personal devotion guide for further help.

Second, LOST Lessons can be used as a small group study. It is designed to help you facilitate an effective small group using the TV show—LOST as a catalyst for discussion of spiritual issues. Use the clips from the show to introduce the topic, the devotions as discussion starters, the scriptures for study, and the small group resources provided for more help. This book is a guide to help you facilitate a small group that draws people to a closer relationship with Christ.

Introduction

Confused, isolated, and stranded; the survivors of Oceanic flight 815 are fighting to survive. In the midst of unknowns and mysteries; they are struggling to find their way, purpose and salvation. Many times in our Christian life we feel like this, we feel lost. We're confused, isolated and stranded; and just like the survivors, we are searching for direction. We struggle to grow close to God and live as He would want us. This book was written to help in this process. It uses the TV show LOST as a catalyst for thoughts, meditations and discussions of spiritual issues. It is designed as a devotional for young adults in hopes that it will be a tool used for spiritual growth. Each devotional contains a summary of a LOST episode highlighting a phrase, issue or theme, and then showing through Scripture how that concept relates to our Christian lives. LOST has changed lives in the area of entertainment, Jesus Christ changes lives today and forever. He offers abundant life (John 10:10) and everlasting life (John 3:16). The authors hope that reading this will encourage a meeting with the Author of life.

The authors in no way advocate or condone the content of the television show LOST; the show is rated at least TV14 and obviously is not suitable for all audiences. As with everything, caution should be used before or during viewing. The authors do not wish this book to be a stumbling block, but a benefit to a relationship with Christ. Do not partake in things that will hinder your walk with God. *"Set your minds on things above, not on earthly things"* (Colossians 3:2). Hopefully, this book will help you learn to view all of life from a heavenly perspective.

NaRul DdaRaORa

Follow Him

Oceanic flight flight 815 departs from Sydney, Australia and is scheduled to land in Los Angeles, California. While in flight, major complications occur; the plane splits in half and crashes on a tropical island. Only 48 survive. Blue waters, sandy beaches and palm trees would normally be an ideal resort-like vacation, but today it is an unwanted detour. Jack, Kate and Charlie decide to go look for the cockpit, find the transceiver and actively seek rescue. As they are planning their mission, a Korean couple comes into view. The night is falling. It has been a long day. People are still scrambling. Uncertainty and fear are roaming throughout the survivors. Jin looks at his wife and says— NaRul DdaRaORa. The closed caption reads—Follow me. Is Jin insecure and doesn't want to be alone? Or is he confident, loving and protective of his wife? The answer is not clear.

Jin continues—You must not leave my sight. You must follow me wherever I go. Dirty, scared, confused and still in shock, Sun nods in agreement. It appears they don't speak or understand English and none of the other survivors understands Korean. Therefore, they better stay together; there is no one else to whom they can communicate. One can feel all alone even though there are people all around him. Jin demands that Sun follow him.

Jesus often offered for others to—Follow Me. Most immediately refused Him by ignoring His offer. To not answer is often to answer. In this case by not saying yes with their feet, they were expressing rejection by standing still and saying nothing. Some refused by making excuses. One put Jesus off by wanting to wait until his father died (Luke 9:59). When his father finally dies, will he use the excuse that he has to care for his mother or run the family business? Maybe he was afraid that his father would disown him. This was a common punishment for those who left their Jewish upbringing. Whatever the reason for his excuse, by putting Jesus off he was saying—No. Another put Jesus on

**Episode 1:
Pilot Part 1**

hold by saying that he first wanted to go back and be sent off by his family (Luke 9:61). Family is important, but that delay was also a denial of Jesus' offer. Finally, one just looked away because he thought the offer was too costly (Mark 10:21). The offer may seem expensive, but to reject the Son of God leads to eternal bankruptcy.

However, a few took up His offer immediately. Levi (better known as Matthew) heeded His call—After this, Jesus went out and saw a tax collector by the name of Levi sitting at his tax booth. Follow me,'Jesus said to him, and Levi got up, left everything and followed him (Luke 5:27-28). Matthew had a job making good money; his life was probably very comfortable, and he had no apparent needs. Yet, at the calling of Jesus he followed. He wasn't concerned about his money or his booth. His only concern was to follow. Likewise, brothers Peter and Andrew jumped aboard—As Jesus was walking beside the Sea of Galilee, he saw two brothers, Simon called Peter and his brother Andrew. They were casting a net into the lake, for they were fishermen.

"Come, follow me, Jesus said, and I will make you fishers of men. At once they left their nets and followed him (Matthew 4:18-20). To leave one's nets behind sounds pretty definite. It would seem acceptable to first clean the nets and put them away, but the brothers chose a new direction in their lives at once. Matthew, Peter and Andrew immediately took up the charge to—Follow Me.

Jesus extends the calling to all believers in Matthew 28:18-20:—Then Jesus came to them and said, All authority in heaven and on earth has been given to me. Therefore go and make disciples of all nations, baptizing them in the name of the Father and of the Son and of the Holy Spirit, and teaching them to obey everything I have commanded you. And surely I am with you always, to the very end of the age.'" Jesus invites all of us to follow Him.

What is God calling you to do today?

_____

_____

_____

_____

What gifts, talents and interests do you have and how could they be used for God?

_____

_____

_____

_____

_____

Have you considered going on a short term missions' trip?

_____

_____

_____

_____

Who has God placed in your life who doesn't know Him yet?

_____

_____

_____

_____

_____

What is your next step (invite them to church, give them a Christian book, share your story in a letter, e-mail or verbally) and when will you do it?

_____

_____

_____

_____

_____

Jesus gives some basic ingredients for following Him daily—Then he said to them all: *"If anyone would come after me, he must deny himself and take up his cross daily and follow me"* (Luke 9:23). Matthew left everything and followed Jesus. Peter and Andrew at once left everything and followed Jesus. They denied themselves and followed Him. Denying involves our talk and walk, our attitude and actions. Everyone is aware of Peter—denying Jesus three times by Peter's claim to have had no association with Him (Luke 22:54-62). However, we miss Titus 1:16—They claim to know God, but by their actions they deny him. They are detestable, disobedient and unfit for

doing anything good. Our words and actions are a testimony of who Jesus Christ is. We need to make sure it is a positive presentation.

Do your words and actions testify that you have taken the call to follow Jesus?

_____

_____

_____

_____

_____

What speaking sins (gossip, swearing, sexual innuendo, lying) do you need to eliminate from your life?

_____

_____

_____

_____

_____

What sinful actions (stealing, alcohol, drugs, cheating) do you need to eliminate from your life?

_____

_____

_____

_____

_____

As LOST goes on, we see that Sun battles with her choice as to whether or not she will wholeheartedly follow Jin. We need to stand firm with Joshua and announce—*As for me and my household, we will serve the LORD* (Joshua 24:15). I will follow Jesus! When God picks you on His team, it is not to sit the bench!

**When God picks you on His team
it is not to sit the bench!**

—Author Unknown

Every Trek Needs a Coward

Fear Not

Jack Kate and Charlie leave the other survivors on the beach as they look for the plane's cockpit. Upon arrival at the cockpit, Jack, Kate and Charlie find only the pilot alive. Almost immediately, a—monster reaches through a broken window, grabs the pilot and kills him. Jack takes the transceiver and the three scouts frantically run for their lives while the monster comes after them. Charlie falls and gets his foot tangled on some vine. Jack comes back and frees Charlie's foot. In the panic the three get separated. Upon

their reunion, Kate asks Charlie what he was doing back at the cockpit in the bathroom. Although he really went back for his heroin, he tells her that he was throwing up. Charlie then shamefully confesses—Every trek needs a coward, and readily admits his fear.

Kate herself had faced fear only moments earlier. All alone in the dreaded woods her steps are frozen by fear. It was then she remembers Jack's approach to fear. While Kate was stitching a huge cut on Jack's back, Jack recounted facing fear early in his medical residency. He told how he gave fear 5 seconds to run its course and then he went back to work, and everything turned out fine. In the middle of the woods and fear, Kate counts, 1—2—3—4—5, and everything turned out fine, fear is a very active—monster. All too often we feed it our emotions and imagination. David had many Goliaths in his life, yet he appeared to have a secret ingredient. It is clear that a definite mindset on God is everything. In one of the most famous passages of all time, David writes—*Even though I walk through the valley of the shadow of death, I will fear no evil, for you are with me; your rod and your staff, they*

comfort me (Psalm 23:4). As a shepherd boy David knew danger first hand. Sheep were a tasty treat for bears and lions. Yet, he had experienced God's deliverance from danger and fear. He fought the beasts with confidence and success. When David became an adult, fear was still near by. David ran for his life from King Saul and hid at En Gedi. This hide out had several caves built into the mountains on both sides of a valley. Saul and his mightiest men were after one man; David was the fugitive. The goal was not to bring him back alive. He was a wanted man, a wanted dead man. As David hid in the caves and peeked out, he truly looked at a valley of the shadow of death. But Psalm 42:1 shows David didn't see fear; he saw deer—As the deer pants for streams of water, so my soul pants for you, O God. David's greatest goal was not to escape Saul, but to be found worthy by God. The closer the enemy came, the closer David sought to be to God. Fear didn't take him prey, it made him pray.

David didn't fear because he knew God was with him. Later he asks rhetorical questions—The LORD is my light and my salvation—whom shall I fear? The LORD is the stronghold of my life—of whom shall I be afraid? (Psalm 27:1) Knowing God means one doesn't really have to know fear. Finally, David gives a statement of triumph that we

No God,
Know Fear
Know God,
No Fear

all want to encompass—I sought the LORD, and he answered me; he delivered me from all my fears (Psalm 34:4). That is an amazing declaration: the Lord delivered David from all his fears.

List three of your biggest fears.

_____

_____

_____

_____

What would be the worst case scenario if your fears became reality?

_____

_____

_____

_____

People have a variety of fears today. Studies and anecdotal confessions show that public speaking may be fear number one for most people. However, private speaking to that someone special can be just as intimidating. When those communication encounters arise we need to remember that God wants to deliver us from all our fears. We are encouraged in 1 Peter 5:7—Cast all your anxiety on him because he cares for you. We need to allow God into our daily lives with its fears as well as its victories. Paul gives clear direction when counting to five isn't enough—Do not be anxious about anything, but in everything, by prayer and petition, with thanksgiving, present your requests to God. And the peace of God, which transcends all understanding, will guard your hearts and your minds in Christ Jesus (Philippians 4:6-7). Prayer brings peace.

Do fears get in your way of being a witness for Christ?

_____

_____

_____

What fear keeps you from witnessing more (rejection, being teased, not knowing the answer to a potential question)?

_____

_____

_____

Write out a prayer specifically asking God to strengthen your faith in Him and for deliverance from the fear.

_____

_____

_____

_____

_____

I remember as a child fearing an open closet, a closed shower curtain, and—something under the bed. With my heart beating I would run up the stairs fearing not only what was in the basement, but what might be under the stairs waiting to grab my ankle. However, fear disappeared when I was with my dad. My dad was my hero; he could conquer anything and definitely that certain—something. With age I have realized that my heavenly Father is always with me. This brings security, comfort and confidence. Every trek may need a coward, but God is willing to make sure it isn't one of His children. Fear Not!

If your knees knock, kneel on them.

Sign outside a London church during

World War II:

Everyone deserves a...

Forgiveness

The Marshal is dying with a piece of shrapnel sticking out of his chest, yet frantically tries to warn Jack that some lady is dangerous. This seems to be a persistent concern when finally he tells Jack to check his jacket pocket. Jack finds a piece of paper that has a police mug shot of Kate. Kate is the dangerous woman. Kate is the fugitive. In the midst of all the drama, Kate has flashbacks of being in Australia. She remembers being on Ray's farm. When she finally left his farm, Ray pretended to drive her to the train station, but instead was turning her into the police for a $23,000 reward. He apologized and she understood. At that point he made a touching statement. He said—Everyone deserves a fresh start. That is the theme and title of this

Episode 3:
Tabula Rasa

episode: Tabula Rasa. It means clean slate. It is the idea of erasing a marker board totally clean, so it shines white as new, no marks or stains.

Episode three ends as Jack and Kate have a closing dialogue. Kate says—I want to tell you what I did – why he was after me. However, Jack replies—I don't want to know. It doesn't matter. Kate, who we were—what we did before this, before the crash. It doesn't really—3 days ago we all died. We should all be able to start over. Everyone does deserve a fresh start.

God offers a fresh start. Acts chapter nine records the transformation of Saul, the persecutor of Christians, to Paul,

the persecuted one for Christ. After the Lord's enlightening visit with Saul on the road to Damascus, God called on Ananias. This was not Ananias the high priest who belittled Paul (Acts 23-24). Nor was it the Ananias who lied to God, and along with his wife Sapphira, was struck down (Acts 5). They lied and died. No, this Ananias was different. He was open and honest with God. God told him that he was to go to the house of Judas and meet with Saul of Tarsus. In Acts 9:13-14 Ananias openly called to the Lord and said, *"I have heard many reports about this man and all the harm he has done to your saints in Jerusalem. And he has come here with authority from the chief priests to arrest all who call on your name."* It is almost as if Ananias expected the Lord to be surprised, to be unaware and to maybe even change His plans. Instead, God comforted Ananias by saying He had a special plan for Saul. Saul would suffer, but he was a chosen instrument by God. God forgave Saul and gave him a clean slate.

Paul shared his testimony in Acts 22:13. In describing Ananias' role, Paul said—He stood beside me and said, 'Brother Saul, receive your sight! And at that very moment I was able to see him. What a beautiful statement. It  says that Ananias stood beside Paul. God forgave Paul and Ananias forgave Paul.

Matthew chapter eighteen contains what is often referred to as the Matthew 18 principle. If someone wrongs us we should first go directly to them. If repentance isn't present then we should take a witness. If the individual still chooses to live in sin we should take it to the church. The goal isn't church discipline; the goal is repentance, reconciliation and a fresh start. People all too often emphasize discipline (3 verses) and miss the emphasis on forgiveness (15 verses). Matthew 18:21-22 is clear that we need to continually forgive others (translated as 77 times in NIV, 490 times in KJV). It really isn't an option. We need to give them a fresh start and a clean slate.

Who has wronged you; who do you need to forgive?

_____

_____

Pray asking God to help you forgive them and for wisdom to know how to stand beside them.

_____

_____

How should you now treat them?

_____

_____

It is difficult to forgive others; however, it is often even more difficult to forgive ourselves. First John 1:9 reminds us—If we confess our sins, he is faithful and just and will forgive us our sins and purify us from all unrighteousness. God will forgive us. We need to accept His forgiveness. Jeremiah goes as far as to say that the Lord will forgive our sins and forget them (Jeremiah 31:34). He will not remember our sins. I like to think of a paper shredder as the forgiveness machine. My sin is like an IOU on a piece of paper. When I confess my sin to God, He takes the paper and puts it through the shredder. He will never use it against me; never rub it in my face. The IOU is eliminated.

Do you have unconfessed sin in your life?

_____

_____

Pray now asking God to forgive you and for wisdom to know how to turn from this sin in the future.

_____

_____

What plans can you now confidently pursue now that you have accepted God's forgiveness?

_____

_____

_____

_____

Micah paints a beautiful picture—Who is a God like you, who pardons sin and forgives the transgression of the remnant of his inheritance? You do not stay angry forever but delight to show mercy. You will again have compassion on us; you will tread our sins underfoot and hurl all our iniquities into the depths of the sea (Micah 7:18-19).

The Lord forgives us and throws our sins into the deepest parts of the sea. We need to post a sign—No fishing! We need to accept God's forgiveness, leave the past alone and press on with a fresh start and a clean slate. God approves that everyone deserves a fresh start.

"Forgiveness from others is charity; from God, grace; from oneself, wisdom."

—Author Unknown

Don't tell me what I can't do

God's Call, Make a Difference

J ohn Locke pulls out a case full of knives and is ready to hunt wild boar for dinner. During the adventurous hunt, four conversations reveal not only Locke's physical state, but his emotional drive as well. First, in a flashback to his work place, Locke and Randy have words. It appears Randy always likes to get under Locke's skin. Randy finds Locke's—Walkabout papers. He tells Locke he can't do it. Locke responds with the name—Norman Croucher. Locke continues that Croucher had no legs and climbed to the top of  Mt. Everest. He refers to—Destiny and then says—Just don't tell me what I can't do. Second, when Michael gets hurt Kate states that they all need to head back to camp.

Locke refuses and says that he would continue the hunt. Kate says—John, you can't. Locke emphatically replies—Don't tell me what I can't do. Third, in another flashback Locke has an intimate phone conversation with Helen. He tells her—I'm free to do all those things I ever wanted to do. Things that I know I was destined to do. Fourth, in the final flashback, Locke and an agent argue over Locke's physical disability – being wheelchair bound - preventing the adventure. Locke yells—You don't know who you're dealing with. Don't ever tell me what I can't do, ever. This is my destiny. This is my destiny. This is my destiny. Finally, he closes with—Don't tell me what I can't do. Don't tell me what I can't…

Locke had a definite—Can Do attitude. He was focused and determined. A silly wheel chair was not going to imprison him. He liked to overcome insurmountable odds. The obvious Bible story that resonates with this episode involves a youngster named David and a monster named Goliath. Although the

kid had less equipment, less size and less experience, he entered the arena with confidence and won. This event occurred 1,000 years before Philippians 4:13 was written, but David believed—I can do everything through him who gives me strength. David knew he had the Lord on his side, or better yet, he knew he was on the Lord's side. That mindset gave him a—Can Do attitude.

God wants us to see the BIG picture. In 2 Kings Chapter six the Arameans were at war with Israel. Elisha's servant saw the enemy all around the city. There was no sign of hope, so he was afraid. Elisha comforted him by revealing that their army was larger. The servant was understandably confused. The Lord opened the eyes of the servant and he saw the hills full of horses and chariots of fire. The servant's vision was enlarged. At the request of Elisha, the Lord struck the enemy with blindness. Not only did God enlarge their army, He also weakened the enemy. Elisha and servant walked away safe, free and with a new perspective.

Where do you feel defeated in life?

_____

_____

_____

Pray asking God for wisdom and confidence as to how to approach the situation.

_____

_____

_____

What three steps do you need to take in becoming victorious?

_____

_____

_____

God has placed a calling on each of our lives. He puts an urgency or desire within us to make a difference in our world. Often we make excuses ignoring or outright rejecting God's invitation to service. God went out of His way to call Moses to lead all of Israel. When God called out to Moses, he answered—_Who am I?_ (Exodus 3:11) Moses had no confidence, he felt inept. God gave the best response—I will be with you (v. 12). God called Moses, but didn't hang him out to fail. He was willing to go with him. Moses needed more convincing. God had Moses' staff turn into a snake and back to a staff; then his hand went into his cloak and came out leprous and then restored. These miracles were still not enough. In Exodus

4:10 Moses gives a weak excuse—*O Lord, I have never been eloquent, neither in the past nor since you have spoken to your servant. I am slow of speech and tongue.* In Acts 7:22 Stephen gives a death bed sermon which includes a description of Moses;—Moses was educated in all the wisdom of the Egyptians and was powerful in speech and action. Moses was a trained, powerful speaker; yet, he told God he couldn't speak. Even if Moses couldn't speak, God reminded him that He was the one who gave man a mouth. God controls sight and sound, the blind and the mute. He was willing to give Moses the words that would be needed. Still Moses whined and pleaded for even more help. Finally, God offered Moses a partner in Aaron. God lead the two men so they could lead His people.

"Confidence is when you care to send
the very best, and you go yourself."

—Robert Orben

Do you have what it takes?

Testing

It's been six days on the island, and things are getting difficult. Their hopes of a quick rescue are dwindling, personal conflicts are increasing in intensity, strange things continue to happen, and on top of it all, they're running out of water. As the reality of life on the island sets in, the natural search for a leader begins and fingers are pointing to Jack to make the big decisions. But Jack is scared. His Dad has constantly told him—You just don't have what it takes to make the tough decisions. Now everyone is looking to him for

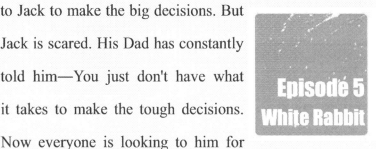

answers, it's his chance to show what kind of character he possesses. In the jungle, exhausted and frustrated, Jack and Locke sit down and talk. Locke challenges Jack, he says the survivors are—Thirsty, Hungry, waiting to be rescued. And they need someone to tell them what to do. Jack replies—I'm not a leader...I don't have what it takes. Locke knows it's clear that Jack is the leader. He must overcome his fear and past to make a decision, will he step up and do what he knows is right? Do you have what it takes?

In his life on the island and as a doctor, Jack is put in the position where he must make life or death decisions; but does Jack—have what it takes? Does he have the character to make difficult choices? Does he have the moral courage and determination to decide to do what he knows is right? In our lives, we are constantly faced with situations where we see if we—have what it takes? Do we have the character to stand up for what we know is right? Do we have the faith to trust in Christ and his ways?

What type of difficult situations are you faced with?

_____

_____

_____

_____

What moral decisions do you make every day in your life?

_____

_____

_____

The Bible is full of examples of people who are force to make decisions that test their character and faith. Some decisions are public where the pressure is increased by the observation and judgment of friends or co-workers. Others are made in private where it becomes simply a battle of will. One man who continually had his character and faith tested through the decisions he made was Daniel. Taken from his family and country and forced to serve as a slave in a work environment that, to put it very mildly, valued a different morality than his (Daniel 1:1-4), Daniel faced situations where his character would be challenged through the very public decisions he made. Not only would he face decisions that would result in the loss of friendships, missed advancements

CHARACTER

at work, and personal freedom; but possibly the loss of life. In Daniel chapter one, he and his friends choose to follow God's commands instead of taking the easy road and fitting in with everyone else. His decisions to follow God even lead his friends to do the same in Daniel chapter 3 despite the prospect of losing their lives. Daniel's public decisions were not luck or coincidence. His public character and decisions were forged from the decisions he made in private. Daniel 6:10 tells us that despite his demanding schedule of ruling a country and a decree that would prohibit him—Three times a day he got down on his knees and prayed, giving thanks to his God, just as he had done before. Daniel made the tough decisions in his private life and built the Godly character it takes to make the hard decisions in his public life.

Our lives are a constant question of—Do we have what it takes? God is constantly putting us in situations where are character and faith are tested through the decisions we make. Character is not made in difficult situations, that's where it is shown. At work/school and in public, our character is shown through our decisions. At home and in private our character is built through our developing relationship with Christ.

In this episode when Charlie is talking with Claire, we can see a tattoo on Charlie's left shoulder that reads—Living is easy with eyes closed. Maybe you're living your life like this; letting opportunities pass you by; afraid, like Jack, to take on the challenges and decisions you face every day that test and prove your character. God is calling all of us to strengthen our relationship with him and build Godly character in our private lives. Every day we spend developing a relationship with Christ we decide what's important and how we are going to live. In doing this, we create the personal faith and strength to stand for him and make the right decisions no matter what the situation. The question is; do you have the character to make the difficult decisions for God? Do you have the moral courage and determination to decide to do what you know is right? Do you have what it takes?

What are some of the moral decisions you are constantly faced with in your public life?

_____

_____

_____

What are some spiritual decisions you are constantly faced with in your private life?

_____

_____

_____

List some areas where you have been making Godly decisions.

_____

_____

_____

List some specific areas where you have you been failing to make Godly decisions.

_____

_____

_____

List 3 ways you can develop more of the personal character required to make the right public decisions at which you have been failing.

_____

_____

_____

What are 3 actions you are going to take this Week in your private life to develop a better relationship with Christ and a stronger Godly character?

_____

_____

Name another person in the Bible who made personal and public decisions to follow the Lord, what were the decisions and what were the results?

_____

_____

_____

Read through the book of Daniel. Where else in Daniel's life did he demonstrate personal and public Godly Character? Ex. Chapter10

_____

_____

_____

_____

_____

_____

_____

"One's philosophy is not best expressed in words. It is expressed in the choices one makes. In the long run, we shape our lives and we shape ourselves. The process never ends until we die."

— Author Unknown

6

Where would you stay?

Priorities and Compromises

The last episode ended with Jack's inspirational speech. He said—We have to stop waiting. We need to start figuring things out...We need to figure out how we're gonna survive here. In episode six, the survivors are forced to decide on their priorities for life on the island. They have the two choices. The first option is that they can go to the caves for safety giving up hope of rescue and resigning to life on the island. Or they can stay on the beach keeping the signal fire going waiting for a rescue but leaving themselves open and exposed to all the dangers of the island. Each survivor is forced to look into themselves to find what's truly important to them.

**Episode 6
House of the
Rising Son**

Jack and a group give up on the thought of being rescued and decide to move into the caves. While Kate and the other half stay on the beach open and exposed waiting for rescue. Each group makes compromises for the things they think are important.

Dealing with priorities and compromises is inevitable; it's a major part of life. Something always takes first place while everything else gets pushed to the side. It seems that no matter what our situation, we always find time and money for the things we really value. The real question is; where do your priorities lie? Are you compromising the world for God, or are you compromising God for the world? (temporary/physical for the eternal/spiritual?)

What things do you currently compromise on in your life?

At work or school

_____

_____

At home and with friends

_____

_____

God's word clearly expresses that His desire is that we set Him as our number one priority (Deut 6:13-19). It is God's longing that we serve him and keep him first; it's everything else that should be compromised. However, in this culture of fast food and instant entertainment it's easy to become divided. Jesus is completely right in Matthew 6:24 when He says—No one can serve two masters. Either he will hate the one and love the other, or he will be devoted to the one and despise the other. You cannot serve both God and money. In our culture, we could substitute many things for—money: TV, self, friendships,

sports, sex, culture, family, fitting in, work, or school. Our days are so busy; we have many demands our time. Often we find God's desires being compromised in our lives. One of the great characters in the Old Testament is Moses. You might remember many great stories from his life, confronting pharaoh, crossing the red sea, getting water from the rock, and the 10 commandments. But when Moses is mentioned in Hebrews 11 along with the other great men of faith, he is remembered for putting God above all else. No matter what the situation, Moses had the right priorities. It says of Moses in Hebrews 11—He chose to be mistreated along with the people of God rather than to enjoy the pleasures of sin for a short time. He regarded disgrace for the sake of Christ as of greater value than the treasures of Egypt, because he was looking ahead to his reward. Moses had his priorities straight and because of that; God was able to use him in spectacular ways.

Each survivor on LOST made concessions for the things they deemed important; we are no different. We always find time for the things that are really important to us. It's amazing how when we have a sports game on Sunday morning

PRIORITIES

we always manage to get up and make it on time; but if it's just church, we might only make it half the time. How many hours a day do you spend in front of the television or on the computer, versus how much time we spend in God's word and prayer. When we get up to get ready to go in the morning, we think it's crazy to walk out the door without finding time to fix our hair, but somehow we never have time for the Lord. What does that say to the Lord about our priorities? It says that sports, television, computers, and even the state of our hair are more important to us than He is. Somehow after all the compromises we make in our relationship with Him, we still expect God to fulfill all our wishes exactly when we want. God wants to be at the center of our priorities. We need to put God first, and live accordingly. You always have to compromise something, what's it going to be, the world or God?

In an average week, how much time do you spend on the following activities:

In front of the television _____

On the computer _____

Getting dressed _____

On the phone _____

Playing video games _____

Playing sports _____

Talking with friends _____

Praying _____

Reading the Bible _____

Witnessing to the lost _____

Write down your top 10 list of priorities for your life, no matter what the situation or time.

_____

_____

_____

_____

_____

_____

What are 3 practical ways that you can make God more of a priority in your life tomorrow?

_____

_____

_____

What are 3 things that need to be compromised in your life?

_____

_____

_____

Is/should God be a higher priority in your life than your family?

_____

_____

_____

Do you need to ask God's forgiveness for not putting Him first?

_____

_____

_____

_____

_____

_____

_____

"The key is not to prioritize what's on your schedule, but to schedule your priorities."

—Stephen R. Covey

The struggle is nature's way of strengthening it

Strengthen Faith Through Trials

Every time the survivors turn around something's wrong: the plane is floating into the sea, people are hurt, kidnapped, missing, or battling with their past. Dealing with the past seems to be a growing pattern in their lives and this episode is no different. Sayid and Kate are attempting to pinpoint the location of the mysterious radio signal. Jack is trapped in a cave struggling to survive and the main story centers around Charlie's fight with his drug addiction. Locke is in possession of Charlie's drugs and gives him three chances to ask for his drugs; the first two times Locke will deny Charlie the drugs, but on the third request Locke will give Charlie the

Episode 7
The Moth

drugs. The second time Charlie asks for the drugs, Locke tells him about the moth. He says—You see this little hole? This moth's just about to emerge. It's in there right now, struggling. It's digging its way through the thick hide of the cocoon. Now, I could help it, take my knife, gently widen the opening, and the moth would be free. But it would be too weak to survive. The struggle is nature's way of strengthening it.

Maybe you were under the false assumption that when you became a Christian, your life would become easy. Unfortunately, this is almost exactly opposite of what happens. Salvation brings with it peace, purpose, eternal life in heaven, and the love of God; but it also brings with it trials. Our Christian life is full of the tests and tribulations of God's design, and just like the moth's struggle, they are intended to strengthen us for what's ahead.

God does not hide the fact that he strengthens our faith in Him through trials; he has used this method from the beginning. Almost every character in the Bible, from Abraham to the disciples, deals with one of the most powerful kings of all times and was a—Man after God's own heart, (1 Samuel 13:14) he did not get that way overnight. King David had firsthand experience at God's strengthening through trial. He said in 1 Chronicles 29:17—I know, my God, that you test the heart...and David understands it well. At a very young age, David knew that God had chosen him to be king, but his days as a ruler were a long way off. God had him live through years of intense hardship before he ever took the crown. He was torn away from his best friend, driven from his home and family, hunted like an animal, with armies trying to kill him. But it was through these trials that God strengthened him and developed the faith and perseverance he would need when he became king. An old saying states that if God's going to do something, He starts with hardship, if he's going to do something great he starts with a catastrophe.

Although we might not have trials on the same scale as David, God uses the same principle in our lives. 1 Peter 1:6-7 says—In this you greatly rejoice, though now for a little while you may have had to suffer grief in all kinds of trials. These have come so that your faith-of greater worth than gold, which perishes even though refined by fire-may be proved genuine and may result in praise, glory and

Refined By Fire

honor when Jesus Christ is revealed. Peter clearly says God uses trials so that our faith, through refining fire, may be strengthened and proven genuine for the glory of God.

The moth's strengthening struggle to escape the cocoon is a great picture of our spiritual lives. God places trials in our path in order to strengthen our faith. He uses difficulties and temptations to build in us a desperate need and love for him. As we deal with the trials, the more we pass the more he sends, strengthening us over and over, building our faith for the great things he has ahead. Even if we fail, God is always there to help us back up and lead us on.

To build physical strength, we must tear apart the muscle that is there. To shape and mold metal, it must be heated and pounded into submission. To get gold pure, it must be refined in the intensity of fire. For the moth to have the strength it needs, it must struggle from the cocoon. For us to have the strength of faith and perseverance required to live a sold out life for Christ, we must go through trials. But don't fear, God gives us a great promise in James

1:12—Blessed is the man who perseveres under trial, because when he has stood the test, he will receive the crown of life that God has promised to those who love him. What could be better than that?

How are you standing up in the trials of your life? Are you developing bitterness? Are losing your struggle? Are you fighting against God? Proverbs 24:16 says—for though a righteous man falls seven times, he rises again, but the wicked are brought down by calamity. Don't be discouraged, don't get downhearted, and don't fear; for we know that God has—plans to prosper you and not to harm you, plans to give you hope and a future (Jeremiah 29:11).

What specific trials is God putting you through on a daily basis?

_____

_____

How are you handling these?

_____

_____

Is there a better way to deal with these trials?

_____

_____

_____

What trials is God putting in your life on a large scale?

_____

_____

_____

How are you dealing with these?

_____

_____

_____

Is there a better way to handle them?

_____

_____

How can you help another Christian who is going through difficult trials?

_____

_____

What can you do to keep your focus on the big picture?

_____

_____

_____

"Fiery trials make golden Christians"

— Author Unknown

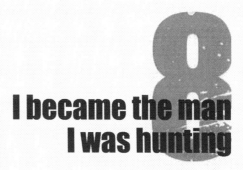

I became the man
I was hunting

Trapped In Sin

On the—deserted island full of unfamiliar people, everyone gets a fresh start. Their past is essentially erased. They get to decide who and what they want to be. But for most of the survivors, the past cannot easily be forgotten. Who they are and what they have done leaves deep scars. Sawyer is definitely no exception. In episode eight, as survivors fight over scraps left from the crash, Sawyer is again confronted in his life with doing what he knows is right or acting in the wrong. Although he has been driven his whole life by a quest for vengeance on the man who destroyed family, Sawyer becomes exactly like the man he has hated. The only way Sawyer

**Episode 8
Confidence
Man**

knows how to deal with this is to make sure that everyone hates him. As Kate discovers the truth behind Sawyer's actions and confronts him on his life, Sawyer says—How's that for tragedy, I became the man I was hunting

In our lives, we constantly find ourselves in a fight between right and wrong. We constantly fail to follow God and find ourselves doing what we don't want to do. God calls believers to be to be holy, and to follow him, but this is no easy task. We are locked in a constant fight between what we know is right and what we actually do.

How is your struggle going?

_____

_____

How are you doing in your personal battle?

_____

_____

The continual struggle in our Christian walks is between knowing the good and doing the good. We want to do what is right, but our body seems not to respond. Even the apostle Paul struggled in this area. He discusses it in the well know passage in Romans 7:15-16; where he says—I do not understand what I do. For what I want to do I do not do, but what I hate I do.

Paul puts it another way in Galatians 5:17—For the sinful nature desires what is contrary to the Spirit, and the Spirit what is contrary to the sinful nature. They are in conflict with each other, so that you do not do what you want. But we do not have to be prisoners to sin; we can overcome the sinful nature through Christ. Paul gives us reassurance of this in Romans 8:13-15 when he says—*For if you live according to the sinful nature, you will die; but if by the Spirit you put to death the misdeeds of the body, you will live, because those who are led by the Spirit of God are sons of God. For you did not receive spirit that makes you a slave again to fear, but you received the Spirit of sonship. And by him we cry, Abba, Father.* Through Christ, we can overcome our sinful nature. Setting our minds on what the Spirit desires, we can triumph. Romans 8:5-6 directs us that—Those who live according to the sinful nature have their minds set on what that nature desires; but those who live in accordance with the Spirit have their minds set on what the Spirit desires. The mind of sinful man is death, but the mind controlled by the Spirit is life and peace.

Many times in our Christian walk we find ourselves saying the same thing as Sayid said after torturing Sawyer—What I did today…I swore I'd never do again. Our minds may be aware of what is right, but our flesh is eager to respond to sinful desires, and unfortunately we frequently find ourselves praying for forgiveness for the same recurring things. If were

not careful, our sinful natures can take over and all types of sin can creep into our lives destroying our testimony and blocking our relationship with the Lord.

Thankfully, we do not have to be trapped by sin. The desire for sin in our lives is strong, but God and His Spirit are infinitely more powerful. In Christ we have freedom from condemnation and access to the amazing power of His Spirit. We cannot defeat the flesh on our own, but when we are controlled by the Holy Spirit; His power is enough to give us victory. Phil 4:13 says—I can do everything through him who gives me strength. Avoid those things that lead you into sin, meditate on the scriptures, actively seek what is right, and focus on the Sprit. Don't let sin turn you into what you detest, use His strength to serve Him.

List 5 things you struggle with on a continual basis.

1. _____

2. _____

3. _____

4. _____

5. _____

Why do you struggle with these things?

_____

_____

_____

What does—living by the Spirit look like?

_____

_____

_____

_____

_____

_____

What 3 things should you do in the next week to—live by the Spirit?

1._____

2._____

3._____

In what specific area's do you need to fight your sin nature?

_____

_____

_____

Who can you develop accountability with in order to help you fight the flesh?

_____

_____

_____

_____

_____

_____

"Do not bite at the bait of pleasure, till you know there is no hook beneath it."

—President Jefferson

You deserve a break, Today!

Stress

Sayid left the group and searched for the source of the French transmission. Along with his backpack was a picture of Nadia and a note. Sayid found a cable. He followed the cable and ended up getting caught by Danielle, the French woman. She questioned him about her lost daughter Alex. Sayid, the torturer, became Sayid, the tortured. Sayid repaired her music box and then used the tool to escape. Taking a faulty gun, he was soon captured, but released with blessings. Meanwhile, Hurley strived to relieve the tension by building a two-hole golf course.

Episode 9
Solitary

Early in the episode, Sullivan came to Jack concerned about his rash. A lot of arguing was present in the background. Jack asked Hurley—What's going on out there? Hurley answered—you know, the usual—people yelling at each other over nothing. Jack explained that Sullivan's rash was brought on by stress. The doctor's prescription was—Just try to relax; it'll clear up; Try to keep your mind off it. Hurley mocked Jack—Try to keep your mind off it? What else has that guy got to do but stress? He continued—We're all fried. I'm mean, have you taken a look at everybody out there? Everybody's way tense. Dude, I'm just saying, it'd be sweet if we could have, I don't know, something to do. Hurley noticed that everyone needed a break.

God knew people would collect stress and need a break. Instead of hoarding stress, we need a release valve. He didn't just design a fifteen minute coffee break, He scheduled one day a week for rest. Exodus 20:8-11 clearly lay out God's plan for our rejuvenation, *"Remember the Sabbath day by keeping it holy. Six days you shall labor and do all your work, but the seventh day is a Sabbath to the LORD your God. On it you shall not do any work, neither you, nor your son or daughter, nor your manservant or maidservant, nor your animals, nor the alien within your gates. For in six days the LORD made the heavens and the earth, the sea, and all that is in them, but he rested on the seventh day. Therefore the LORD blessed the Sabbath day and made it holy."* God sent the example by creating all of creation in six days and then taking a day of rest. He then emphasizes the point by demanding a day of rest as number four of the Ten Commandments. Of all the instructions needed for civilizing cultures, God pointed out that man needed a day to get refreshed and revived emotionally, physically, mentally, and of course spiritually.

How can a small group Bible study revive someone emotionally?

_____

_____

_____

A walk in the woods taking in the fresh air can bring life to many. What is a great way for you to become physically refreshed?

_____

_____

_____

Mentally revived doesn't mean think of nothing. What book have you been wanting to read, but can't fit it into your schedule?

_____

_____

_____

Psalm 46:10 starts out—Be still, and know that I am God. Do you do all the talking in your relationship with God?

_____

_____

_____

When will you schedule time to—be still?

_____

_____

_____

Solomon noticed the downward spiral of man—All his days his work is pain and grief; even at night his mind does not rest. This too is meaningless (Ecclesiastes 2:23). We tend to fret, worry, stress-out, and get anxious. In Psalm 62:1 David said—My soul finds rest in God alone; my salvation comes from him. Hopefully, Solomon saw others panic while his dad, David, prayed. David knew to take time and rest with God. This is not just an Old Testament concept. Hebrews 4:9-11 continues the lifestyle—*There remains, then, a Sabbath-rest for the people of God; for anyone who enters God's rest also rests from his own work, just as God did from his. Let us, therefore, make every effort to enter that rest, so that no one will fall by following their example of disobedience.* To ignore a day of rest is to be disobedient to God.

Are you being obedient to God?

_____

_____

Are you willing to become obedient in all ways?

_____

_____

Describe an ideal (and affordable) day of refreshment.

_____

_____

What is keeping you from scheduling that day?

_____

_____

Later in episode nine Kate approached Jack while he was golfing. She made a very telling statement when she said—I almost didn't recognize you. You're smiling. Rest and relaxation can take many forms, but the outcome leads to joy. Many quote Philippians 4:4 on the topic of joy—Rejoice in the Lord always. I will say it again: Rejoice! Few realize that Paul stated this from prison. We love to rejoice when all is going well, but Paul tells us to rejoice at all times. This is easier when we obey God and rest. Remember Proverbs 17:22 says—A cheerful heart is good medicine, but a crushed spirit dries up the bones. Jack needed to take the Doctor's orders to rest and enjoy life. Your schedule may include school, sports, music lessons, projects and work. Do you believe there is no time to rest? Is your plate a little too full? Do you feel life is overwhelming and there is no escape? Reevaluate priorities and elevate the position of rest.

What items are mandatory in your weekly schedule?

_____

_____

What items should be eliminated from your weekly schedule?

_____

_____

When will you schedule time to—be still and know He is God?

_____

_____

A little rest can lead to joy and God's best. The Great Physician knows that you deserve a break, Today. And He does mean day.

"Some of us would do more for the Lord if we did less."

—Vance Havner

Adoption: A Chosen One

Family of God

Claire hears a baby crying. She is having horrible nightmares, flashbacks, an attack and even contractions. She recalls first finding out she is pregnant. She has three choices: start a family, abortion or adoption. Her and her boyfriend, Thomas, decide to give family a try. A friend convinces Claire to go to a psychic. Malkin, the psychic, sees something disturbing and refuses to give Claire a reading. After a few months, Thomas changes his mind. He selfishly feels he is not ready to settle down. Thomas walks out on Claire and their baby.

Episode 10
Raised By Another

Claire goes back to Malkin. She intends giving her baby up for adoption, but Malkin insists that she must raise this child herself or danger will result. She runs out, but he is persistent with phone calls. Malkin has an alternative plan. Claire joins a lawyer and meets with a family to sign adoption papers, but at the last moment she changes her mind. She goes back to Malkin to hear his plan. Malkin offers her money and a plane ticket to fly to Los Angeles and give her baby to a different adopting family with whom her baby will be safe. The flight she is to take has to be Oceanic flight 815. Did the psychic know the future and send Claire and her baby to their death?

It is God's desire for everyone to be spiritually pure. God forbids the use of a psychic. Too many souls are lost through curiosity in the dark side. Leviticus 19:31 says—*Do not turn to mediums or seek out spiritists, for you will be defiled by them. I am the LORD your God.* Leviticus 19:26 bluntly finishes by saying—Do not practice divination or sorcery. Deuteronomy 18:10-11 is more specific as examples are listed—*Let no one be found among you who sacrifices his son or daughter in the fire, who practices divination or sorcery, interprets omens, engages in witchcraft, or casts spells, or who is a medium or*

spiritist or who consults the dead. God does not want people defiled by Satan and his realm. It was wrong for Claire to go to a psychic.

It is God's will for everyone to be sexually pure. 1 Thessalonians 4:3-5 says—*It is God's will that you should be sanctified: that you should avoid sexual immorality; that each of you should learn to control his own body in a way that is holy and honorable, not in passionate lust like the heathen, who do not know God.* Everyone can control their own body. 1 Timothy 4:12 challenges youth to be an example including purity—*Don't let anyone look down on you because you are young, but set an example for the believers in speech, in life, in love, in faith and in purity.* Finally, 1 Timothy 5:2 reminds men to treat—younger women as sisters, with absolute purity. It was wrong for Claire and Thomas to be sexually active with each other without being married to each other.

However, this episode depicts a scene that is all too common today. Claire was faced with three choices: start a family, abortion or adoption.

ADOPTION IS AN OPTION

Many people today know the reality of that dilemma. Many people today should be grateful their parents (married or not) decided to keep the child. All too often adoption has a negative connotation; however, this is not true in Scripture. Scripture paints a comforting family portrait of adoption as one is chosen to be part of the family.

Mephibosheth was a crippled child nobody wanted until one special day. Mephibosheth was Jonathan's nephew. All of Mephibosheth's family had been killed including Uncle Jonathan. Mephibosheth's life could be in jeopardy if certain people realize he was related to Saul. Things looked very glum. Then it all changed in one special day. King David was missing his best friend, Jonathan. He wanted to do something special in honor of Jonathan. He asked, *"Is there anyone still left of the house of Saul to whom I can show kindness for Jonathan's sake"* (2 Samuel 9:1)?

Someone singled out Mephibosheth. David insisted that Mephibosheth—will always eat at my table (2 Samuel 9:10). The very next verse climaxes that one special day—So Mephibosheth ate at David's table like one of the king's sons. Mephibosheth was adopted by David. He ate at the king's table. He was family. Being a child of the king has benefits. He changed from that crippled kid nobody wanted into a child of the king. That was one special day.

Ephesians 1:3-5 describe that one special day for Christians—*Praise be to the God and Father of our Lord Jesus Christ, who has blessed us in the heavenly realms with every spiritual blessing in Christ. For he chose us in him before the creation of the world to be holy and blameless in his sight. In love he predestined us to be adopted as his sons through Jesus Christ, in accordance with his pleasure and will.* God chose us. He adopted us. We are His children. Being a child of the King has benefits. Since we are God's children—*Let us then approach the throne of grace with confidence, so that we may receive mercy and find grace to help us in our time of need* (Hebrews 4:16). God calls us His child. We can go talk to Dad anytime we want. We are His pride and joy. We should talk to Him often about everything and anything. Nothing is too big or trivial to Him. Say it—I am a child of the King!

Thomas and Claire are frantic when they first realize she is pregnant. The unspoken multiple choice question is prevalent:

start a family, abortion or adoption.—D – All the above is not an option. In the death threatening tone of the moment, Thomas says—Hey, Claire? If we, if we wanted to, we could do this. He goes on to say—This could be like, uh, I don't know. It could be like the best thing ever. Life is the right choice. God is able to turn sour grapes into sweet tasting wine. Adoption can be the best thing ever. For the Christian, being adopted by God is the best thing ever.

If you have accepted Christ as Savior, write out a short prayer thanking God for adopting you as His own child.

_____

_____

_____

_____

If you are not secure about your eternal future and your relationship with God, write out a prayer expressing your need of God and requesting that He adopt you now.

_____

_____

_____

The choice is simple – you can either stand up and be counted, or lie down and be counted out.

— Author Unknown

Not on the list

Salvation

Claire Not on the list and Charlie are missing. Hurley has been working on a census of all the survivors and realizes something is wrong. Ethan is not on the list. Hurley was using the passenger manifest and noticed that Ethan is not on the list. It is believed that Ethan has abducted both Claire and Charlie. Sayid told them there were others on the island when he got back from Danielle. Could Ethan be one

Episode 11
All the Best Cowboys
Have Daddy Issues

of the others? Locke, Boone, Kate and Jack are tracking the trail of the missing trio. Charlie's finger tape's trail leads into two directions. The scouts split into two groups. Jack encounters Ethan. Ethan gives Jack a pounding and a death warning. It is now clear Ethan is the enemy. Jack and Kate ignore the threat and press on. They find Charlie hanging and dead. Through rigorous moments Jack revives Charlie. The three of them head back to camp. Locke and Boone continue their fruitless search until they find something in the ground. The object is large and made of steel.

Ethan Rom was not on the list. Have you ever experienced the feeling of not being on a special list? Maybe it was the Honor Roll or Dean's List that you were hopefully scanning. Or it could have been a Friday afternoon when the Varsity roster is posted for all to see. It could even be those chosen for a special project/assignment at work. Being on the list can be one of the greatest feelings ever.

Write out a time you remember when you made the list.

_____

_____

How did it make you feel?

_____

_____

Who did you immediately tell?

_____

_____

Write out a time you remember when you weren't on a list.

_____

_____

Did it make you try harder for the next time?

_____

_____

Did it turn out negative or positive that you weren't on the list?

_____

_____

Gideon had to make some cuts to downsize his troops. The book of Judges tells us that Israel had 32,000 soldiers (7:3) while the Midianites had 135,000 swordsmen (8:10). The odds didn't look good and God wanted to make it seem impossible. He told Gideon to let everyone go home who—trembles with fear. Twenty-two thousand left. That means it is 10,000 against 135,000. God said Gideon still had too many men. The final decider was how they drank water. If they lapped the water with their tongue like a dog they were sent home. Nine thousand seven hundred were sent home. The final list was three hundred men. Now it is 300 against 135,000. This is literally life and death. Chapters seven and eight record how God performed the miracle and the three hundred were victorious. It would have been so cool to be on that list.

Is God calling you for a project where the odds seem insurmountable?

_____

_____

Write out how you feel God wants to use you now.

_____

_____

_____

_____

_____

The Bible also talks about the greatest list ever. It is the Lamb's Book of Life. Revelation 20:15 states—If anyone's name was not found written in the book of life, he was thrown into the lake of fire. God has a special book. It records everyone who is going to Heaven. If you are not in the Book you don't get in to Heaven. You don't want your name blotted out of this book (Psalm 69:27-28). God wants you to know that your name is on the list. First John 5:11-13 says—And this is the testimony: God has given us eternal life, and this life is in his Son. He who has the Son has life; he who does not have the Son of God does not have life. I write these things to you who believe in the name of the Son of God so that you may know that you have eternal life. God has clearly shown the way of salvation that we may—know that we have eternal life. We may not know the future, but we know who holds the future and He has a grip on us.

What friends are you worried are not yet in the Lamb's Book of Life? _____

_____

What will you do now to start to reach them?

_____

_____

_____

Jack had several flashbacks during this episode of him and his—under the influence father failing to save a lady's life in surgery. Jack's father accepts the fact that you just can't save them all. Today, we need realize that not everyone is or will be saved. There is a Hell and the majority of people have a one way ticket on that flight. Make sure you are on the right flight.

Write out when you accepted Christ as Savior.

_____

_____

_____

Sawyer finds out that Sayid is back from his journey. Sayid had tortured Sawyer miserably earlier. Now it could be Sawyer's turn. As Sayid explain his remorse, Sawyer responds—Sorry, fresh out of sweet forgiveness. It can be common for us to feel that we just can't be forgiven. We have gone too far away. We have crossed the line too many times. There is no hope. This is not true of God. He has an endless supply of sweet forgiveness. Accept His love and gift of eternal life. Make sure your name is in the Book of Life. Make sure you are on the list.

Some people dream of worthy accomplishments, while others stay awake and do them.

— Author Unknown

12

The Key

We Need Others

Kaye and Sawyer are looking for more fruit trees when they find a beautiful swimming hole and something else. Deep within the lagoon are remains of the crash and a special silver case. Sawyer is trying everything to pick the lock on the silver Halliburton case. Jack and Kate have to dig up the Marshal to get the key from his pocket. Kate is having numerous flashbacks of a bank robbery she orchestrated. The case is opened. Inside are four guns, ammo, some money and a small envelope marked—personal effects. All Kate wants is the little green envelope. It contains a small toy airplane. It belonged to the man she loved and killed.

Episode 12
Whatever the
case may be

Meanwhile, people are moving camp as the tides rise. Locke and Boone pretend to search for Claire as they go to the steel container all day, every day. Sayid asks Shannon to translate the French notations. After much agony she finally realizes the notes are only lyrics to a beautiful song—La Mer. Shannon sings the song in French.

Early in the episode Kate is deep in the woods when she hears some movement in the brush. She throws a rock and ends up hitting Sawyer who had been following her. He agonizes and she asks why he is following her. Sawyer says—Yeah, well, you shouldn't be out here alone. Kate gives an emphatic—I'm fine. I can take care of myself. Sawyer mockingly projects—Oh, of course. I don't need protection. I can take care of myself. Me Kate. Me throw rock. It is ironic that on this island it should be observed that—no man is an island.

The mindset that I can take care of myself is healthy to an extent, but we need to realize that God has placed us together for each other. We need each other. Paul writes in 1 Corinthians  12:12—*The body is a unit, though it is made up of many parts; and though all its parts are many, they form one body. So it is with Christ.* Believers need to realize that we are all part of something much bigger than ourselves. Paul goes on to challenge the—I'm fine, I can take care of myself mindset in 1 Corinthians 12:21—*The eye cannot say to the hand, I don't need you! ' And the head cannot say to the feet, I don't need you!'''* We need each other. God has placed the pieces together in such a way that we shouldn't isolate ourselves and hibernate. It can be tempting to give up on everyone else. People will disappoint us. It is well known that if you want something done right – do it yourself. Yet, we need to learn that we need others. Ecclesiastes 4:9-10 paints a healthy dependency—*Two are better than one, because they have a good return for their work: If one falls down, his friend can help him up. But pity the man who falls and has no one to help him up!*

List some people you know you can depend on.

_____

_____

Pray thanking God for them.

_____

_____

_____

_____

How do they know they can count on you?

_____

_____

Sayid is a trained self-sufficient warrior, yet he realizes he needs help. He goes to Shannon and says—I need a favor. I need your help. Now, Shannon has just been reminded by Boone that she is worthless. Sayid asks her for help. He needs her to translate the French papers he took from Danielle. Teamwork seems to be God's plan as far back as Adam and Eve. In Mark 6 Jesus sent the twelve disciples out two by two and in Luke 10 He sent the seventy-two followers out in pairs. It is important to work together.

What are your greatest interests and talents?

_____

_____

Who could help you develop those more?

_____

_____

What is a major weakness for you?

_____

_____

Who has God placed nearby who is strong in this area?

_____

_____

Why are you hesitant to ask for help?

_____

_____

Throughout the episode Rose chooses to interact with Charlie. She first tells him she needs his help moving her belongings down the coast. Later, she comforts him by pointing out that no one blames him for Claire's kidnapping. He responds that it may have been better if he would have died. Rose says—You know what I think, Charlie? You need to ask for help. Charlie inquires—Who's going to help me? Finally, at the end of the episode Charlie reaches out to Rose and pleads—Help me. Rose turns Charlie's initial dependence from herself to God and prays—Baby, I'm not the one that can help you...Heavenly Father, we thank you. We thank you for bringing us together tonight, and we ask that you show Charlie the path... First, we need to realize that we need God. There is a void in our lives that can only be filled by Him. Next, we need to realize that as a believer we are a needed member of the Body of Christ. We need to contribute. Finally, as one of many parts in the Body, we need to let others contribute. We are a team.

Typically, it is difficult to ask for help because people throw it back in our face. They may help, but they hold it over us. We feel worse for asking. God doesn't do this. James 1:5 emphasizes God's generous and kind disposition—If any of you lacks wisdom, he should ask God, who gives generously to all without finding fault, and it will be given to him. He could be little us, yet He gives without finding fault. He gives without criticizing us. He gives without making us feel like nothing.

It appears from Michael and Hurley that the Halliburton is an impressive case. However, this amazing shiny silver case could not reach its full potential without the simple, flimsy, seemingly insignificant key.

God cares for people through people.

—— Author Unknown

Time to let go

Things We Put Before God

For most of the survivors on the island this episode is comparatively light and uneventful. Hurley, desperate for some protein, seeks Jin's help in catching some fish. In the process he has a painful meeting with a sea urchin, but makes a friend in Jin. While Kate is helping Sun with the garden and enlisting Jack's help, she uncovers the secret of Sun's ability to speak English. However, in this episode one survivor has a life shattering experience. Lock and Boone continue to head off into the jungle in secrecy to figure out how to open the hatch they have discovered. Boone is reluctant to do what is necessary to open the hatch and keep it a secret, he is constantly held

Episode 13
Hearts and
Minds

back by his concern/love for Shannon. Pressured by his sisters budding romance with Sayid and her questions about his activities, Boone is convinced he must tell her about the hatch, but Lock has different plans. After being drugged and tied up by Lock, Boone has an experience where he sees his -sister die, and he soon realizes he must choose between his love for Shannon or following Locke.

Just like us, Boone's life changing experience comes when he finally makes a decision about his priorities. Its only when he is willing to let go is he able to fully follow. In our lives we all have things that we hold on to, priorities that pull us in all different directions. The value we put on earthly things constantly turn us away from being committed to God. If you want to follow God completely, as Locke says, it's—time to let go.

Looking at the time you spend on different things throughout the week, what are your top 5 priorities?

What would you like your top 5 priorities to be?

_____

_____

_____

_____

God desires that we be wholly committed to Him; he doesn't want the part left over after we've finished with all our other priorities.

He wants to be foremost in our life. Jesus said in Matthew 22:37-38 that we are to—*Love the Lord your God with all your heart and with all your soul and with all your mind. This is the first and greatest commandment.* The first thing we should do as Christians is to put God first and love Him completely. It doesn't say to love him with the leftover parts of your heart, soul and mind. Jesus even goes so far as to say *"If anyone comes to me and does not hate his father and mother, his wife and children, his brothers and sisters-yes, even his own life-he cannot be my disciple* (Luke 14:26). Obviously, Jesus isn't advocating hate; but he is making it clear that nothing, not even our families or the value of our own lives, should come close to being a priority over His desires. Jesus is saying, we should be so committed to God that it seems like we hate everything else in comparison with our love and devotion to Christ. There's an old saying that goes—If Jesus isn't Lord of all, He's not Lord at all.

Like Boone's desire to open the hatch, we often find our desire for following God getting choked out by other things. Matthew 13, Mark 4, and Luke 8 all tell the parable of the sower, a parable describing the conditions of our hearts in relation to God and his message. In the parable, Jesus describes a seed that has fallen among thorns; the plant grew, but was

 eventually choked out by the thorns around it. Jesus explains this part of the parable in Matthew 13:22—*The one who received the seed that fell among the thorns is the man who hears the word, but the worries of this life and the deceitfulness of wealth choke it, making it unfruitful.* Does this describe your faith and life? Are things in your life choking out your willingness to follow God? Do you need to weed out some thorns so you can follow God and be productive for Him?

Maybe you're like the rich young man in Matthew 19 whose desire for wealth keeps him from fully following God. Or maybe you're like the man in Luke 9 who put his family before following Jesus. Or maybe you're like Peter, disowning Jesus at the crucifixion in Matthew 26, where basic fear is keeping you from God. Whatever your thorns are, they won't leave by accident, on their own, or just because you go to church. You don't grow closer to God simply because you want to; you must take personal action, you must make conscious decisions about your faith. Growth requires putting in the time and effort of getting to know Him and to learn more about Him.

You must intentionally take the steps necessary to put God first and everything else a very distinct distant second.

Whatever your placing over God, your job, your status, your desire for popularity, your need for personal success, or maybe something as simple as personal entertainment; whatever it is, you need to lay it at God's feet, set your priorities and intentionally live them. It's—time to let go of our selfish desires and take action to follow God completely.

What are 3 thorns you have that are choking out your spiritual life?

_____

_____

What actions do you need to take to get rid of these—thorns

_____

_____

What 3 things can you do this week to make sure that God is first in your life?

_____

_____

_____

_____

_____

_____

_____

_____

_____

_____

_____

It is the mark of great people to treat trifles as trifles and important matters as important.

—Doris Lessing

"He seems to hate it" "What?" "Being a dad"

God As Our Father

It's been about a week and Clair is still missing. Charlie's fear for her and regret for letting her get captured grows everyday. After an internal moral battle, Charlie's curiosity gets the best of him and he begins to read Clair's diary. But he's not the only one on the island stressing. Michael continues to be frustrated about his relationship with Walt, and they seem to fight at every turn. He feels very threatened and angered by Walt's relationship with Locke. After a near fight, Michael forbids Walt from having any contact with Locke. Michael is fed up and convinced he must be proactive at getting off the island. He must build a raft. However, Walt keeps running off, and

Episode 14 Special

it eventually takes a team effort of Locke and Michael to save him from a polar bear.

As the flashbacks show, Michael's fatherly relationship with Walt is a complicated one. Although he is the biological father, he has never been Walt's father. Although Michael has always had the intention of being a great father for Walt, his efforts seem to fail at every turn. Walt has never known a true father.

Maybe you're like Walt. Have you grown up with an errant view of what a father is? Maybe to you, a father is someone who simply works, comes home and watches TV, or someone who fixes the car, or someone who has never around, or someone who is abusive. Don't confuse earthly fathers with your heavenly Father. Although the Bible frequently uses the picture of the fatherhood of God, no earthly father, no matter how good they are, could ever match up to God.

If you are saved, you are adopted into God's family (Ephesians 1:5), and you can be assured that—*You are all sons of God through faith in Christ Jesus.* (Galatians 3:26) God is our Heavenly Father and He takes on this

role actively. He acts as the perfect Father for us. He exercises his care and providence over us (Matthew 6:26, 7:11). He shows us compassion and love (Psalms 103:13, 2 Corinthians 1:3). He is our creator and sustainer (1 Corinthians 8:6, Acts 17:24-25), He will commune with us (Exodus 25:22), he knew us before we were born (Jeremiah 1:5). God provides for our needs and security (1 Timothy 6:17, Ps 91:14), He blesses us (Matthew 7:11), He is faithful (Hebrews 13:5) and He never changes (Malachi 3:16). And like every good father, He also disciplines and corrects (Deuteronomy 8:5, Hebrews 12:5-6). He is our heavenly father and we are his children (2 Corinthians 6:18). Although earthly fathers may fall short, God never does. Matthew 7:11 reminds us that—*If you, then, though you are evil, know how to give good gifts to your children, how much more will your Father in heaven give good gifts to those who ask him!*

How would you describe your relationship with your earthly father?

_____

_____

How do you think that has affected your view of God as your Heavenly Father?

_____

_____

God as our father is a great picture of the relationship He desires to have with us. Although God is the creator and sustainer of all life, the God of infinite power and infallible wisdom  and holiness, he chooses to be our father. When you think about it, this is amazing. The fact that the author of all life desires to have this type of relationship with us is incredible. The Lord of all wants to develop such a deep relationship with us that we would call him Father.

Why would God bother to portray himself this way? What does it change in your life that God is known as, not just as your God, but your Father? Really think about it; because it makes a difference, and it means some wonderful things for us. First, as our Father, we have access to God. We have the potential to get to know him, to develop a relationship. God as a Father also means that we have access to his resources. His power, His strength, his knowledge is available for us. It also means that God desires to see us reach our potential for him. We can trust that the things he gives us, the things he allows us to go through are for our good and for the purpose of seeing us glorify him.

How would things change for you if someone famous, like the president or a rich, famous actor, said they wanted to be your father figure? It would change your entire life. God wants to be your Father; He is reaching out, trying to connect, trying to direct and teach us, and trying to develop a relationship. Are you open? Are you ready to be a child of God? Are you willing to take hold of your inheritance? Are you prepared to represent the family?

How would you describe your relationship with your Heavenly Father?

_____

_____

What needs to change on your part to develop a better relationship with God?

_____

_____

How are you representing your Heavenly Father?

In your relationships?

_____

_____

_____

At your work or school?

_____

_____

_____

In your use of money?

_____

_____

_____

In your family?

_____

_____

_____

_____

_____

"A man knows when he is growing old
because he begins to look
like his father."

—Gabriel Garcia Marquez

Under Attack

Satan's Attack

The survivors are under attack, they're scared, on edge, and for good reason. After Locke finds Clair in the woods and brings her back to camp, she can't remember anything. But that doesn't stop Ethan from coming after her. Ethan attacks Charlie and Jin in the woods and demands that Clair be brought to him or he will start killing. This sends fear through the camp, and the survivors begin to develop a defense system. As Locke, Sayid and Boone put up a warning system in the jungle, the rest of the group hunkers down in caves.

However, the defense has a huge hole, during the night Ethan sneaks in through the water and kills one of the survivors. After the death and urging from Kate, Jack decides to get out the guns and the survivors set a trap for Ethan. The trap works, but he isn't in their custody for long. Charlie, driven by his failures to protect in the past, shoots and kills Ethan to protect Clair.

The poor survivors, they never get a break. It seems like every second their being attacked by something. If it's not polar bears, boars, or the black cloud, then it's the Others. Do you ever feel like life just keeps hitting you with struggle after struggle and you can't catch a break? You feel like you're under attack and maybe someone's out to get you? That's because there is. Someone wants you to lose heart, to step away from your faith and keep you thinking all is futile.

Has there been a time in your life when you felt like everything was against you? Describe it.

_____

_____

_____

_____

_____

Who did you blame for this? What did that do to your spiritual life?

_____

_____

_____

The Bible makes it very clear that as Christians, we are always under attack, and its more than just bad karma and chance. Ephesians 6:12 says—For our struggle is not against flesh and blood, but against the rulers, against the authorities, against the powers of this dark world and against the  spiritual forces of evil in the heavenly realms. There is a very real war going on and Satan will use any means necessary to oppose the gospel and its messengers. Attacks and persecution are not a rarity, it's part of being a Christian. We should expect to face oppression and hardships on account of our faith.—Infact, everyone who wants to live a godly life in Christ Jesus will be persecuted. (2 Timothy 3:12) There is a real battle going on, and if we step out for Christ, we will most certainly be attacked.

Unfortunately, these assaults from Satan often achieve his goal of bringing discouragement, fear, and a loss of faith in Christ. However, these attacks should not pull us away from God, as

they often do, they should draw us closer. If we understand we are in a battle and realize the enemy and their goal, hardship should not draw us away from Christ; it should draw closer to Him. When facing difficulties and persecution we draw on His power and cling tighter to His promises and salvation. In times of attack, we find our strength and assurance in Christ.

The disciples were fully aware of the attacks of Satan. They were repeatedly ridiculed, exiled, beaten, thrown in jail, and stoned. And most ended up dying as martyrs for Christ. Acts 5:41 is a great example of their attitude towards the attacks by Satan—*The apostles left the Sanhedrin, rejoicing because they had been counted worthy of suffering disgrace for the Name.* Our attitude towards the attacks of Satan should not be fear and a loss of faith; we should consider it an honor to be associating with the creator of the universe. Remember the words of 1 Peter 4:16—*However, if you suffer as a Christian,*

do not be ashamed, but praise God that
you bear that name.

Maybe you're reading this and you cannot relate. Your life is simple, refined and you don't feel like your being attacked. Is that because you are not stepping out for God? Have you grown complacent and are in no danger of furthering the gospel? Don't let Satan win, fight back and step up for the cause of Christ.

If you are standing up for God and are under attack, don't pull away, draw near to Him and rely on his might and authority. Fight with courage (1 Corinthians 16:13), determination (1 Timothy 6:12), watchfulness (1 Peter 5:8), and prayer (Ephesians 8:18). Put on the full armor of God (Ephesians 6:11), and do everything you can to stand. Don't go quietly into the night, realize you're in the battle, use the strength from the Lord, and never stop fighting.

"The Lord is my light and my salvation,
whom shall I fear?
The Lord is the strength of my life; of
who shall I be afraid?"

—Psalms 27:1

"I never carried a letter around for twenty years because I couldn't get over my baggage"

Justified Through Christ

Also most every episode on Lost deals with survivors who are struggling with their past; fighting choices made before the plane crash. In this episode, as Charlie is dealing with killing Ethan, we get to see a little more of the dark and mysterious past of the man the survivors know as Sawyer. In the flashbacks we see that having become what he hates, Sawyer is making his way through life conning women, as a confidence man. Until an associate shows up, claiming to have found the man that conned Sawyers parents and ultimately leads to their terrible deaths. Sawyer heads down to Australia and kills him, only to find out he was tricked, it wasn't the

Episode 16
Outlaws

man who destroyed his family, he was deceived into doing someone else's dirty work.

"I never carried a letter around for twenty years because I couldn't get over my baggage"

On the island, Sawyer is constantly overwhelmed by hate and aggression. He is constantly picking fights, purposely angering people, and just being downright malicious. He despises who he is and what he has become. Sawyer cannot escape the guilt from becoming what destroyed his family and from murdering the wrong man. His choices have taken a toll on Sawyer and his guilt is destroying him.

Is there guilt in your life that is keeping you captive? Describe it:

_____

_____

What is guilt doing to your life and relationship with God?

_____

_____

We all feel guilt at one time or another, because we all are guilty; anybody perfect? We all have things in our past we know make us guilty. The shame and remorse can be paralyzing. But we can get past it; our guilt doesn't need to limit or keep us from living for Christ.

In the Old Testament, people removed their guilt and condemnation through the sacrificial system. There were all kinds of offerings, sin offerings (Numbers 15:27) and offerings for fault removal on the Day of Atonement (Leviticus 16:20). There was even a specific guilt offering (Leviticus 6:6-7), done so that people could be—forgiven for any of these things he did that made him guilty. However, ultimately the sacrificial system was insufficient (Hebrews 10:1-4). As Hebrews 10:4 explains they were not adequate—because it is impossible for the blood of bulls and goats to take away sins. Not only that—the gifts and sacrifices being offered were not able to clear the conscience of the worshiper. (Hebrews 9:9) There needed to be a better way.

When Jesus came to earth, he changed everything; He came as the sacrifice that was sufficient. His perfect life, death, and resurrection became the sacrifice for our sins (Romans 5:9).

As John 1:29 says, He became the—Lamb of God, who takes away the sin of the world! His sacrifice was permanent and sufficient for all sins (Rom 8:1; 5:9; 1 John 1:7-9). Christ's death provided the means for the removal of our guilt, through His sacrifice we are acknowledged innocent before God. Our justification is like a legal declaration by God that we are found not guilty. (Romans 8:33-34) Our sin no longer condemns us because we are justified through Christ! Amazing!

This justification has two parts. First, when we accept salvation, we receive the forgiveness of sin. Through this, guilt, condemnation and the penalty of sin are eradicated. (Romans 8:1). Not only that, but forgiveness repairs our broken relationship with God. God's forgiveness is incredible and complete. When we are forgiven our sin is totally eradicated, Jesus says—I remember no more. (Jeremiah 31:34).

The second part of justification leaves us not only exonerated, but declared pure. We have forgiveness. Our filth has come away spotless and we have been released from its shame. In addition, Christ purity is given to us (Romans 5:17). In one of the most unfair trades of all time, the refuse and waste of our lives is assign to Jesus, and in return we are given His purity. 2 Corinthians 5:21—*God made him who had no sin to be sin for us, so that in him we might become the righteousness of God.* We have been found guilty, but through Christ, we are innocent.

The amazing gift of God's justification does not mean freedom to sin. We do not get to skip the consequences of our actions. Even though we are forgiven and receive Christ's righteousness, we still must face the cost of our disobedience on earth. We still must deal with the effects of sin and the consequences of our choices in life. Not only do we face the effects of our sin, but our kids, and their kids, and their kids may have to suffer for the things we do wrong. Exodus 20:5 says, that is—*punishing the children for the sin of the fathers to the third and fourth generation of those who hate me.*

But God's goodness is also passed down, Luke 1:50—*His is mercy extends to those who fear him, from generation to generation.*

_____
_____
_____
_____
_____
_____
_____
_____
_____
_____
_____
_____
_____
_____
_____
_____
_____
_____
_____
_____

"Guilt is your refusal to allow Jesus
Christ to pay for your sins. "

—Kent Crockett

17

— God Knows That

Perspective

un is walking along the beach in her bathing suit. Jin starts yelling at her apparently because of her lack of modesty. Michael steps in to protect Sun. Sun slaps Michael in the face. Jin and Sun walk away. Michael goes back to working on the raft. His goal is to get his son off the island. That night the raft is on fire. Michael is furious and knows Jin did it in revenge. He and Sawyer want to find Jin. Sawyer finds Jin, gives him a pounding and is taking him back to the beach. Michael sees Jin and wants to punish him. While he is interrogating Jin with his fists, Sun yells in English for him to stop because Jin did not start the fire; he got hurt trying to stop it. Everyone is startled at her English. No one, including

Episode 17
..In Translation

her husband, expected that she spoke English. Jin and Sun are allowed to walk away. Jin is furious at Sun's longtime deceit and leaves her. Locke and Walt play backgammon as Walt admits he started the fire. Michael is building another raft and Jin volunteers to help.

Flashbacks tell the story behind the story. Jin asks Sun's father for permission to marry his daughter. Permission is granted. Later, on their wedding day, Jin promises a honeymoon in six months.

He must first work for her dad to show commitment. One job is remembered where he warned a man, but didn't hurt him. The man must not have paid attention because Jin was reprimanded by his father-in-law and sent back with a real hit man to deliver a message. The hit man prepares his gun. Jin pounds the man so he won't be shot. When Jin got home, Sun saw her husband's bloody hands and started believing he was evil. Sun plans to leave Jin. The flashbacks close with a heart wrenching conversation by Jin and his dad. All is forgiven. It is time to start over.

Sun slapped Michael. She literally hauled off and smacked him. She later went to him, apologized and explained—When I slapped you I was protecting you. Michael didn't understand.

Sun knew her husband was a professional—messenger. Jin was a man who had had blood on his hands. Michael thought Sun was rude and unappreciative, but she may have saved his life. Jin distributed the same grace earlier when he worked for Sun's dad. As he beats a man, he says—The factory opens tomorrow. I just saved your life. The man, his wife and his little girl didn't know that the man in the white coat was going to shoot him. They didn't realize that—the beating saved his life.

Have you ever been offended or hurt by someone only to find out later they were helping or protecting you? It could happen when you are driving. You may have someone flash his or her bright lights at you. You look and see that your brights aren't on and get a little perturbed at their annoying action. Up the road you find danger or even police radar. Their intention in stinging your eyes may have been meant as a blessing.

List a time that you were offended by someone only to find out later it was for your good.

_____

_____

Was it someone you should have been able to trust?

_____

_____

How did it make you feel?

_____

_____

Did they do it to harm you or help you?

_____

_____

How can you offend someone in love?

_____

_____

Is there someone right now that you need to challenge even though it may hurt his or her feelings?

_____

_____

As children we may not have realized why our parents wouldn't let us spend the night over a certain friend's house. They may have hurt our feelings and even embarrassed us.

However, maybe they knew something we didn't. Later in life, they make us stay at someone else's house because of inappropriate actions and attitude. They kick us out of the house. It is called—Tough Love. It is difficult to accept pain even when it prevents us from bigger problems.

Joseph had amazing perspective. His brothers were jealous of him and threw him in a pit. They were going to kill him, but decided to sell him into slavery instead. Later, after his prison to palace experience, Joseph's brothers worry that he will  now take revenge on them. In Genesis 50:20 he says—You intended to harm me, but God intended it for good to accomplish what is now being done, the saving of many lives. Joseph knew God's plans for his life could not be altered by anyone else. He allowed setbacks and focused on starting over. His attitude took him from the pit and even prison, all the way to the palace.

What set back are you facing now (job insecurity, broken relationship, poor health)?

_____

_____

_____

How could God use this for good?

_____

_____

_____

Michael was so frustrated when he looked at the burnt up raft. He couldn't salvage a thing. He apologizes to Walt. Walt consoles—It's okay. Michael responds with a new perspective—No. Come here. Come here, look, we all have set-backs. I mean, God knows that. It's just life, we'll start over. They start working together.

This episode is entitled—In Translation. When people hurt us, we need to realize they may have had something better for us. We may be inclined to miss translate or interpret their action. Setbacks will come.—God knows that. We need to avoid judging the motives of others and focus more of our energy on starting over.

Isn't it true that we judge ourselves by our intentions and others by their worst fault?

— Author Unknown

18

4 8 15 16 23 42 < 1

One God

Michael, Jin and Hurley are building the new raft. Michael asks Jack for a transmitter to signal a ship while they are out to sea. A battery is needed. Hurley remembers that Sayid mentioned that Danielle had batteries. Sayid does not want to see Danielle again. He shows Jack and Hurley the papers. Hurley sees the numbers 4 8 15 16 23 42. Hurley becomes persistent to find Danielle and understand the numbers.

**Episode 18
NUMBERS**

Hurley had used those numbers and won the lottery: $156,000,000.

He thinks the numbers are cursed. Since he won the lottery his grandpa Tito died, Father Aguillar was struck by lightning at the funeral, Diego moved back home after Lisa left him for a waitress, his mom broke her ankle, her dream house burned, he was arrested as a drug dealer, his sneaker company burned down killing eight people, and then a man fell off the building. Hurley went to the Mental Hospital to see Leonard. Leonard just kept rattling the numbers.

Hurley asked the meaning of the numbers. Leonard panicked and referred to Sam Toomey. Hurley went to Australia to find Sam. He found Sam's place and wife. She mentioned Sam committed suicide because he felt the numbers were cursed.

Hurley leaves to find Danielle. Jack, Sayid and Charlie eventually follow him. Hurley asks Danielle what the numbers mean. Danielle says she doesn't know. Hurley explodes. She agrees the numbers are cursed. Hurley is relieved knowing he isn't crazy. Danielle gives him a battery and he leaves.

4 8 15 16 23 42 are interesting numbers. It would be interesting to know how many people have tried it as a phone number: 481-516-2342. You might want to change your phone number. Are the numbers a countdown to something special? 4 years, 8 months, 15 days, 16 hours, 23 minutes, 42 seconds. Is the countdown the end of the world or the start of

the World Cup? Maybe the numbers are GPS coordinates: Latitude 4.815, Longitude 162.342. The cross arrows do lead to a point in the Pacific Ocean northeast of Australia. Finally, note: $4 + 8 + 15 + 16 + 23 + 42 = 108$ - Maybe that number will eventually appear in Lost.

All this focus on numbers could lead one to wonder—Is 42 really the answer to life, the universe and everything? Is 42 the key number? Is 42 the most important number?

The Bible emphasizes certain numbers: 2 relates to division, 6 is the number of man, 7 shows perfection, 40 means trial, and 666 is definitely something to avoid. However, the most crucial number for today is ONE.

Paul writes in 1 Timothy 2:5—*For there is one God and one mediator between God and men, the man Christ Jesus.* There is only one go between for us and God. There is only One. It is Christ Jesus. There is only One way to God. John 14:6 says—*Jesus answered, I am the way and the truth and the life. No one comes to the Father except through me.* There is only One way to God. It is through Jesus. If there are other ways to Heaven why did God allow Jesus to die? If there are others ways to Heaven God is dumb or definitely unloving. Why would a loving parent allow their only child to die if there was an alternative? Jesus is the only way to the Father and Heaven.

Do all religions basically teach the same thing?

_____

_____

_____

Is it possible for all religions to be correct?

_____

_____

_____

Who is / was Jesus?

_____

_____

_____

Religions definitely vary drastically in their teachings of the Son of God, Jesus. Jesus is the second person of the Trinity and hence is God. He was not created, but came to earth and lived a perfect life for 33 years. He died for our sins, was buried, three days later He rose again, remained on earth for

40 days and ascended to Heaven where He now resides at the right hand of God the Father. He promises to return. However, some view Jesus differently. Buddhism and Scientology find nothing important or special about Jesus. Others simplify Jesus to being just a prophet (Islam), a teacher/guru (Hinduism), or just another created being who is not God and did not physically rise from the dead (Christian Science, Jehovah's Witnesses, Mormonism, Unification Church). And then there are those who conclude everyone is God (New Age).

"If salvation could be attained only by working hard, then surely horses and donkeys would be in heaven."

—Martin Luther

—You and I are here for a reason

Purpose

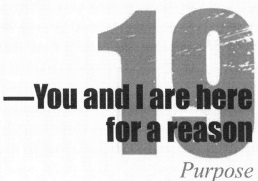

Locke and Boone are trying to open the hatch. They have a large trebuchet set in place. Locke springs the trebuchet, but it doesn't even seem to dent the hatch. Boone points out the piece of shrapnel in Lock's leg. Locke removes it. That night Locke is testing the feeling in his legs. Is his paralysis returning? Lock and Boone try to rebuild the trebuchet. Locke has a vision and then later a dream of a small plane crashing. Meanwhile, Michael and Jin are proceeding quickly on building the new raft; Jack solves Sawyer's headaches with glasses that make him look—like someone steam rolled Harry Potter (Hurley). Locke and Boone are searching for the answer

**Episode 19
Deus Ex
Machina**

to the dream. They find a small plane on a cliff. Nigerian drug smugglers dressed as priests must have crashed on the island much earlier. Boone is climbing the cliff and enters the plane. He finds statues of Mary filled with Heroin. Boone looks at the plane instrument panel and notices the radio. He tries the radio and hears static and a voice. Someone is out there. The plane moves, it is unstable. As Boone tries to transmit, the plane falls and flips over. Boone is seriously hurt. Locke carries him back to camp.

Locke has several flashbacks. They start when he worked in a toy store and meet his biological mother. She had given him up for adoption. Later they have coffee together. He asks about his father. She says he was immaculately conceived. Locke hires an investigator who confirms that Emily is his mother and reveals who his father is. Locke meets his father, Anthony Cooper. Father and son begin to hunt and spend time together. It is revealed that Anthony needs a kidney transplant. Locke volunteers. When Locke wakes up from surgery, his father is gone and his mother shows up. It is revealed that Locke was set up. Emily received money, Anthony received a kidney, and Locke again was alone.

Earlier at the diner, Emily made a statement to Locke that is so powerful. She said—I want to tell you that you're special, very special. You're part of a design. You do realize that, don't you? We are special. We are handmade by God Himself. We should rejoice with David as he praises God in Psalm 139:13-16 saying—For you created my inmost being; you knit me together in my mother's womb. I praise you because I am fearfully and wonderfully made; your works are wonderful, I know that full well. My frame was not hidden from you when I was made in the secret place. When I was woven together in the depths of the earth, your eyes saw my unformed body. All the days ordained for me were written in your book before one of them came to be. God fearfully and wonderfully makes us. He doesn't make mistakes. Each one of us is very special. Don't let the daze of depression lead to days of depression. Remember we are special and we are part of a design. The Lord told Jeremiah, *"Before I formed you in the womb I knew you, before you were born I set you apart; I appointed you as a prophet to the nations"* (Jeremiah 1:5). Before Jeremiah was born, God already had a plan for him. God has a plan for us, too. We are part of His design and plan.

What special talents and interests do you have?

_____

_____

What special circumstances or connections do you have?

_____

_____

How could God use you in a special way?

_____

_____

When Locke and Boone were looking for the small plane, Boone started doubting everything and had some questions. Locke responded—I know it sounds crazy. Four weeks ago I wouldn't have believed it myself. But you and I are here for a reason. We are part of God's design and plan, and are here for a reason. The book of Esther climaxes with this theme. Haman hated Mordecai. Mordecai was Jewish. Haman deceived the king into believing that the Jewish people were against him. The king agreed to have a special day when all Jews could be killed and their possessions taken. However, there was an unknown factor. Mordecai had a niece that he raised as his daughter. She was the queen. Her name was Esther. Esther had never revealed her nationality. Mordecai pleaded for her to get involved. He said, *"Do not think that because you are in the king's house you alone of all the Jews will escape. For if you remain silent at this time, relief and deliverance for the Jews will arise from another place, but you and your father's family will perish. And who knows but that you have come to royal position for such a time as this"* (Esther 4:12-14)? Mordecai knew Esther was part of God's design. She could make a  difference. After prayer and fasting she stepped in and history was written. The Jewish people still celebrate her action as a holiday called Purim. We are here for a reason. God has a plan for our lives. He has placed us next to people in our neighborhood, at school, at work and where we regularly shop that need to get to know Him. God made us special and put us here for a reason; we must take action. James 4:17 is a strong reminder:

Anyone, then, who knows the good he ought to do and doesn't do it, sins. Do you have an inner urge of something you need to do?

_____

_____

What is God calling you to do?

_____

_____

This episode ends with a very heart wrenching emotional cry. Locke pounds on the hatch as he pleads—I have done everything you wanted me to do; so, why did you do this to me? Immediately a light shines from the hatch. This scene portrays the submissive Christian. We do everything we feel God calls us to do. We fully submit to Him. Finally, with patience we see the light.

Emily said to Locke what God says to us—I want to tell you that you're special, very special. You're part of a design. You do realize that, don't you? Knowing we are special and here for a reason, we should start each day praying—God, what are You up to today? Can I be part of it?

Nothing contributes so much to tranquilizing the mind as a steady purpose a point on which the soul may fix its intellectual eye.

—Mary Wollstonecraft Shelley

A Time to be Born, A Time to Die

Death

Boone is seriously hurt. Jack asks Sun to help him. Kate and Hurley are sent on errands to help. Boone's lung collapses. Jack sticks a knitting needle through Boone's chest and temporarily solves the problem. Boone is losing a lot of blood; he needs a transfusion. If things aren't bad enough, his right leg is severely fractured. Jack and Sun forcefully reset it. Now focus is on getting Boone a blood transfusion. A perfect match is hard to find. Shannon, his sister, is not found because she is having a romantic picnic with Sayid. Jack has O negative blood and becomes both doctor and donor for Boone. The transfusion seems to work, but Boone's right leg is

Episode 20
Do No Harm

filling with blood. The leg is dead and has to go. Jack and Michael create a guillotine to amputate Boone's right leg. Sun pleads for Jack to let Boone die peacefully. There is nothing that can be done. Jack is relentless until Boone intercedes and releases Jack of the responsibility of saving him. Boone says—Let me go. There is no hope. Boone concludes—Tell Shannon, tell Shannon, tell… and he dies. Sorrow fills the air.

List the names of some dear friends and relatives who have already died.

_____

_____

What do you miss about them?

_____

_____

How did they impact you?

_____

_____

Are they in a way still impacting you?

_____

_____

While death was making a house call on the island, life was emerging. Kate is returning to the cave with the alcohol, but she hears Claire. Claire is in labor. Kate screams for help. Jin hears the cry and comes to them. Kate sends Jin to Jack with the alcohol and a call for help. Jin finds Jack. Jack refuses to come; he must save Boone. Jack informs Jin that Kate will have to deliver the baby solo. Claire fights the delivery and won't push. Kate convinces her that it will be all right. Claire concedes and a healthy baby boy is born. Mother and baby are fine. Rejoicing fills the air.

Babies are beautiful. It is amazing how a seven pound eight ounce baby can melt a six foot four inch 225 pound linebacker named Junior. A baby can cause any Bubba to squeal—gaga goo goo. A baby entering the world is exciting. Solomon writes in Psalm 127:3—*Sons are a heritage from the LORD, children a reward from him.* Children are a reward. A reward is an honor, a trophy, a blessing. The Message Bible translates the verse—Don't you see that children are God's best gift? Claire struggled with the idea of having a child. She fought labor. Fortunately, Kate was able to help her see that children are one of God's best gifts. His absolute best gift was when

He gave His own son for us. God wants to bless us eternally and daily. We often focus on the gift of salvation and miss His daily local blessings. Children are a blessing from God.

Has God placed a needy child in your life?

_____

_____

What should you do to make an impact in his or her life?

_____

_____

Solomon also wrote—_There is a time for everything, and a season for every activity under heaven: a time to be born and a time to die_ (Ecclesiastes 3:1-2). The natural cycle of life is birth to death, cradle to casket. First Thessalonians 4:13-14 says—_Brothers, we do not want you to be ignorant about those who fall asleep, or to grieve like the rest of men, who have no hope. We believe that Jesus died and rose again and so we believe that God will bring with Jesus those who have_

fallen asleep in him. Death can bring despair, but it doesn't have to last. Salvation brings hope and assurance. Paul states in 1 Corinthians 15:55-57—*Death has been swallowed up in victory. Where, O death, is your victory? Where, O death, is your sting? The sting of death is sin, and the power of sin is the law. But thanks be to God! He gives us the victory through our Lord Jesus Christ.* Death gives everyone a turn, but Christians are victorious in Jesus. Death loses. Psalm 116:15 exalts—*Precious in the sight of the LORD is the death of his saints.* We shouldn't rush death, but it isn't the enemy. We need to make sure our salvation is secure and also that of our family and friends. We can't put off the decision. Second Corinthians 6:2 exclaims—*I tell you, now is the time of God's favor, now is the day of salvation.* Death doesn't make appointments, so now is the day of decision. Take the step of faith with both feet.

"But in this world nothing can be said to be certain, except death and taxes."

—Benjamin Franklin

Motive

Test Your Motives

Much of Lost is based on flashbacks into the former lives of the survivors. We have learned about Charlie's drug habit, Jin and Son's rocky relationship, Michael's new role as a father, Kate's arrest and much more. This episode helps us understand more about Sayid. As we see Charlie struggling with shooting Ethan, we get another glimpse into the former life of a soldier. Sayid driven by his love for a woman must decide between seeing her again and betraying a good friend, who has become a terrorist. Although Sayid

Episode 21
The Greater
Good

helps to stop the terrorist attack, he doesn't do it for—the greater good of Islam or Australia. He does it for his own selfish desires.

One reason the flashbacks are so revealing is because they give us insight into the reasons behind the character's words and actions. Last episode gave us insight into why Charlie would shoot Ethan and this episode we see him dealing with those motives. We also learn a lot more about Sayid and the motives behind his past and current actions of discovering what Locke is up to. The flashbacks help us understand each survivor and the reasons for the things they do on the island.

As Christians our lives can become full of religious action; doing or not doing for a whole variety of reasons. But it is not the action that God is ultimately concerned with, it's our motives. A general principle  in God's morality is that the motives behind an action are as much a determination of right and wrong as the action itself. That's not saying that the end justifies the means, but that God is very concern with the reason behind our actions. (New Unger's Bible Dictionary) When God looks at us, he doesn't just look at the performance or outcome, he looks at the reasons behind it. We often find ourselves judging other people simply by what they do the outward statements they make, but God looks further. Proverbs 20:27 says—The lamp of the LORD searches the spirit of a man; it searches out his inmost being. God is not just concerned with surface action, in the end, God judges us by our hearts. For—*All a man's ways seem innocent to him, but motives are weighed by the LORD* (Proverbs 16:2).

Make a list of the—religious actions you do every week.

_____

_____

What are the motives behind these actions?

_____

_____

Ananias and Sapphira, in Acts 5, are great examples of how important motives are to God. This husband and wife had sold a piece of property and pretended like they gave the whole value to the disciples, but in reality they held back some for themselves. At this Peter says, "*Ananias, how is it that Satan has so filled your heart that you have lied to the Holy Spirit and have kept for yourself some of the money you received for the land? Didn't it belong to you before it was sold? And after it was sold, wasn't the money at your disposal? What made you think of doing such a thing? You have not lied to men but to God.*" God instantly struck dead both Ananias and Sapphira, not because they had to give all the money, but because of their wrong motives.

The apostle Paul is a great example of someone with the right motives. Although he accomplished amazing things in his life, he always wanted pure motives before God. In Acts 14, when people tried to praise him and hail him as a God, Paul tore his cloths and focused their attention on God. Additionally, Paul is famous for these words in Philippians 3:8—I consider everything a loss compared to the surpassing greatness of knowing Christ Jesus my Lord. His purpose, his reasons for action was not for selfish gain, but for God and His glory.

Doing things for the Lord is good, but if done for the wrong reasons they mean nothing.—"*The LORD does not look at the things man looks at. Man looks at the outward appearance, but the LORD looks at the heart.*" (1 Samuel 16:7) Actions by themselves are meaningless; God is concerned with our purpose and reason. He looks beyond our actions and test our hearts and minds (Jeremiah 11:20). The Psalms tell us that God's desire is that we have—truth in the inner parts (Psalms 51:6). 1 Chronicles 29:17—I know, my God, that you test the heart and are pleased with integrity.

God looks not only at the things we do but at why we do them. When you do things for the Lord, make sure it's for the right reasons. Test your motives, God is.

We should often be ashamed of our finest actions if the world understood all the motives behind them.

—Francois De La Rochefoucauld

"You always want to run away"

Running From God

The raft is nearing completion, and the anticipation is growing. But with monsoon season approaching, the raft must leave now. Each survivor has their own feelings about its departure. For Sun, the raft seems to be splitting her marriage. As Jin prepares to leave, the gap between them will become more than emotional. For Michael, the quest to get his son off the island is almost complete. For others, like Charlie, the rafts departure brings a sense of hope and the promise of rescue, but Kate has a whole different set of feelings. Being wanted by the police, the prospect of rescue is not inviting. Her only chance of escape is getting on the raft. But this is not easy,

Episode 22
Born To Run

the raft is full, and after Michael is poisoned, all eyes point to her convict past. But this is not the first time Kate is tried to run away. She has made a life out of it. Even from early childhood we learn that Kate is—born to run; always running away from her problems, always running from the consequences of here actions, always running and hurting those around her.

In our lives running can seem like the best way out. When we face problems and difficult situations it's easier to avoid them. It seems easier to ignore and run from trouble in relationships, it seems better to evade and dodge the consequences of some of our choices; but is that the best option? Is that what will solve problems and bring resolution? Is that how you deal with things in your life—You always want to run away?

What are some of the most difficult things you face in your life?

_____

_____

How do you handle these things on a regular basis?

_____

_____

The Bible is full of accounts of people who try to run from the problems they create. From the first sin of Adam and Eve, humans have tried to avoid their responsibilities. Adam said in Genesis 3:12—The woman you put here with me--she gave me some fruit from the tree, and I ate it." Eve responded by saying—*The serpent deceived me, and I ate.*" (Genesis 3:13). Sarah tried to blame Abraham for her mistake of not waiting on God's promise of a son in Genesis 16:5. Aaron tried to deny his responsibilities after making the golden calf for Israelites (Exodus 32:19-24) and Saul did a similar thing after not following Gods direction in destroying the Amalekites in 1 Samuel 15. Pilate even tried to run from his guilt of sending Jesus to the cross in Matthew 27:24, "*I am innocent of this man's blood," he said. "It is your responsibility!"*

All too often we find ourselves running from obstacles and problems in our lives. We do anything we can to avoid our responsibilities and the consequences of our actions. It's difficult, because running can be a very appealing option. We don't have to face anything or deal with tough situations. However, running is not a biblical option and it always has bad results.

Not only do we run from our problems, we frequently run from what God wants from us. Probably the most famous biblical example of this is Jonah, found in the book of the Bible that bears his name. After receiving a commission to preach in Nineveh, Jonah physically ran in the opposite direction, trying to run from what God wanted for him. After spending what I'm sure was three very long days inside the belly of a large fish, Jonah finally saw the light; you cannot escape the commands or judgment of God. Running does no good; no matter how far or how fast you run consequences always catch up.

Running is not always physical like it was for Kate and Jonah; we can run from God in all different ways. Abraham and Sarah ran from God when they grew tired of waiting on God's promise and had Ishmael with a maidservant (Genesis 16). Aaron and the Israelites ran from God in their lack of faith when they built the golden calf (Exodus 32). David was caught running from God's precepts when he had an affair with Bathsheba then committed murder to cover it up (2 Samuel 11). Peter ran from God when he put his desires before the will of God when he cut the ear off of a Priest's servant when they came to arrest Jesus (John 18:10). Like these characters in the

Bible, our lives are full of places where we have to decide, do I stand and do what I know is right or do I run.

"Courage is not the absence of fear, but rather the judgment that something else is more important than fear. "

—Ambrose Redmoon

Message in a Bottle

The Bible, God's Word for Us

The French woman has come with a startling message, there's black smoke, the Others are coming. She gives them three options, run, hide, or die. This message begins the main plot for season one finale, and rightfully so, the message sends the survivors into a panic. The raft is not quite ready to launch, and with the others coming it must be launched now. It will take Jack rounding up everyone's help to get it into the water before nightfall. Along with launching the raft, the survivors are preparing to hide in the caves; and Jack, Hurley,

**Episode 23
Exodus Part 1**

Kate, Locke and Artz are heading off to find dynamite. Led by the French women, they venture into the Dark Territory, toward the Black Rock to find the means for opening the hatch; but it's no quiet trip. They encounter some type of monster, what the French women describes as a security system, for the island.

While the dynamite expedition continues, the raft is finally ready to launch. All the survivors say their goodbyes, the boat, its four passengers, and the radar system head out into the ocean. The boat contains one more item; something Charlie put together, messages in a bottle. Charlie has collected notes, messages from the survivors in case the raft is found. What would you write for the bottle? What would your message be? If you had one chance, one message to get across, one thing to say to your family, friends, loved ones, and everyone else? What would that be?

The Bible is like God's message in a bottle for us. It's His statement, His—one thing He wants to get across to us. It's His chance to tell us what we need to know. God sent His Son to earth to bring His message to us, and to tell us the most important message for life. That's what the scriptures are, Gods essential message and guidance for us. It may be a long message, and it may have taken several messengers to write, but it's God's direct communication, written specifically for us.

What role does the Bible play in your everyday life?

_____

_____

To what extent does it determine the choices and decisions that you make?

_____

_____

The message of the Bible has two main objectives. First, it's to lead people to salvation. It is through God's revelation of the Bible that we are to know about the soul saving message of the Cross. It is His way of bringing us the Gospel. John 20:31 speaks of the words in the Bible;—But these are written that you may believe that Jesus is the Christ, the Son of God, and that by believing you may have life in his name. The scriptures were written so that we might know God's salvation.

Secondly, the scriptures were written to lead believers to maturity in their faith. The Bible contains what we need to know to learn and grow as Christians. 2 Timothy 3:16-17 says—All Scripture is God-breathed and is useful for teaching, rebuking, correcting and training in righteousness, so that the man of God may be thoroughly equipped for every good work. That's one useful book. The Bible is capable of teaching wisdom (Colossians 3:16)—judging the thoughts and attitudes of the heart (Hebrews 4:12), and providing instruction in the right way to live (Deuteronomy 29:29). It can show us our path (Psalms 119:105), give understanding (Psalms 119:130), provide assurance and encouragement (1 John 5:13, Romans 15:4). It is the Truth (John 17:17). The Bible is the foundation of spiritual growth. It is the tool God has given us for spiritual maturity and understanding. It is the Holy Scriptures—which are able to make you wise for salvation through faith in Christ Jesus. (2 Timothy 3:15-16)

The Bible is God's direct words for us. It is the ultimate authority for our lives, given directly to us, from God. What's more, God's biblical revelation is sufficient and complete (Deuteronomy 4:1-2, Joshua 1:7-8, Proverbs 30:5-6). It's also inerrant (2 Timothy 3:16), pure, (Psalms 12:6), perfect (Psalms 119:96), and true (Proverbs 30:5). God has this incredible message for us, His salvation and the best possible way to live life, and he wrote it down, perfectly, specifically for us. That's awesome!

So why is it not more important to us? Why do we take is so lightly? Why do we set it aside and ignore it? Why do we think of other things when it's read, or fall asleep when were reading it? Has it really sunk in to our hearts and minds what the Bible is? If it really has, would we leave this miraculous message to gather dust on our shelves, dressers and night stands? The Bible is God's salvation and message for us, don't leave it floating in the ocean, pick it up and use it.

"It ain't those parts of the Bible that I can't understand that bother me, it is the parts that I do understand. "

—Mark Twain

"Each one of us was brought here for a reason"

Meaning in Life

I t's —all come down to this, the season finale. Through, desertion, betrayals, fights, survival, polar bears, attacks, boars, injury, monsters, and death, the survivors of Oceanic flight have lived; and now launched a raft. Their hope for rescue is high, but balanced by their fight for survival on the island. As the survivors head out to take shelter in the caves, the French women returns and steals Claire's baby. Sayid and Charlie head out to rescue the baby. Running through the jungle, dodging traps, they finally reach the fire, the French Women, and retrieve the baby. The raft is not having an easy time either, after almost losing the rudder and shooting off a flare, a

Episode 24
Exodus
Part 2

boat of people comes and kidnaps Walt, and burns the raft. The dynamite expedition has made it to the Black Rock; which turns out to be a boat run aground several miles inland. After a horrible catastrophe with Artz, Locke, Kate, Hurley, and Jack bring some dynamite back and blow open the hatch.

While Locke and Jack walk back to the hatch with dynamite, they discuss their differing approaches to life on the Island. Locke points out that Jack is a man of science, and he, a man of faith. Locke says—Do you really think all this is an accident... Do you think we crashed on this place by coincidence... We were brought here for a purpose, for a reason, all of us. Each one of us was brought here for a reason.

Like the survivors we often struggle with the question of purpose. We find ourselves asking the age-old question—Why am I here. No matter who you are, what stage of life you're in, the question cannot be escaped. The question of meaning becomes prevalent when life begins to feel random. When it seems like there's no reason behind anything. In times like these we look for meaning in all aspects of life, wealth, power, education, courage, friendship, love, but none of these bring lasting purpose, they all fall short. Is there purpose and meaning that reaches beyond just trying to make it through the day? Is life just a ride on the random waves of life?

In what situations do you find yourself asking the question—why am I here?

_____

_____

What is your usual answer?

_____

_____

Thankfully life is not just random. It is not just buying time between birth and death. God has created and given us a very real and meaningful purpose. God did not need to create man (Acts 17:24-25) and he needs nothing from us (Job 41:11). However, He did create us, and this gives us security that our lives have importance. We were created for a reason. God created us—in order that we, who were the first to hope in Christ, might be for the praise of his glory. (Ephesians 1:12) We were created  for His glory. We were created for a reason, and that reason is our purpose, to glorify God with every aspect of our lives.

We were also created to take delight in God. John 10:9-10 says—*The thief comes only to steal and kill and destroy; I have come that they may have life, and have it to the full.* The purpose of Life is to bring glory to God and to enjoy God and to take enjoyment in him. In Psalms 16:11 we hear David express—*You have made known to me the path of life; you will fill me with joy in your presence, with eternal pleasures at your right hand.* God created us to bring glory to him, our purpose is to bring him honor, enjoy him, and live with the fullness of that joy.

In life, we can get so caught up in the everyday tasks of life. We can get discouraged by the monotony and the seemingly randomness by which things occur. Be encouraged, life is not random; there is a greater purpose and meaning that comes through our amazing Creator. When we truly realize our purpose, start to act in ways that fulfill it, we can experience a life of joy in the Lord that we have never known before. Don't live life at random, fulfill your purpose.

What are Satan's purposes for your life?

_____

_____

What areas of your life are you allowing Satan to fulfill his Purposes?

_____

_____

Can you think of places in the Bible where God states purposes for you life?

_____

_____

How can you start fulfilling God's purposes today?

_____

_____

I want the whole Christ for my Savior, the whole Bible for my book, the whole Church for my fellowship, and the whole world for my book

——Author Unknown

Study Guide -

*To aid in Group Discussion or to
Personally Look a little
Deeper*

NaRul DdaRaORa

Episode 1 Part 1

Deeper Further study on following Jesus:

People or groups that followed Jesus

Matthew 4:25,	Matthew 20:34
Matthew 9:27,	Matthew 8:23

People who said yes to Jesus' call

Matthew 4:18-20,	Mark 1:19-20
John 1:43-45	

Example of those who faltered in following Jesus

Math 19:21,	Luke 9:59-60

Those who continued to follow Jesus even in suffering

John 13:12-17

Acts 22:4

Romans 15:5

1 Corinthians 11:1

1 Peter 2: 20-23

Jack and Kate discuss finding transceiver

Disc 1, Episode 1 – Time 18:05-20:00

Jin tells Sun—NaRul DdaRaORa (—Follow me)

Disc 1, Episode 1 – Time 17:14-17:39

Every Trek Needs a Coward

Pilot Part 2

Further study on Fear:

God desires his followers to be courageous

    Joshua 1:6-9,   Judges 7:9-11

    2 Chronicles 20:15, 17

Examples of fear preventing people from acknowledging Christ publicly

    John 12:42-43, John 19:38

    Episode 2:

God gives hope to the fearful

    Proverbs 29:25,   Judges 7:10

    Psalms 56:3-4,   Luke 21:12-19

God giving Believers Boldness

Acts 4:5-10,   Acts 13

Acts 29-31

Jack recounts fear

Disc 1, Episode 1 – Time 13:05-15:16

Kate faces fear

Disc 1, Episode 1 – Time 38:00-39:10

Charlie confesses—Every trek needs a coward

Disc 1, Episode 2 – Time 0:00-2:26

Everyone deserves a...

Episode 3 Tabula Rasa

Further study on forgiveness (fresh start):

God's character and forgiveness

Exodus 43:5-7

Nehemiah 9:16-17

Psalms 103:1-18

Isaiah 43:25

1 John 1:8-9

God's pledge of forgiveness

Jeremiah 31:31-34

Isaiah 55:6-7

Hebrews 8:8-12

Means of forgiveness

Old Covenant

Heb 9:22,   Leviticus 4:27-31

New Covenant

Matthew 26:27-28,   Ephesians 1:7-8

Colossians 2:13-15

Assurance of forgiveness

1 John 1:8-9,   Psalms 51:7

Psalms 103:8-12,   Isaiah 1:18

Acts 2:38,   James 5:13-16

1 John 2:1-2

The Marshall states that Kate is dangerous

Disc 1, Episode 3 – Time 1:02-2:05

Ray tells Kate—Everyone deserves a fresh start

Disc 1, Episode 3 – Time 17:42-19:28

Jack tells Kate he doesn't need to know her past

Disc 1, Episode 3 – Time 38:16-39:40

Don't tell me what I can't do

Episode 4 Walkabout

Further study on a—Can Do attitude (power/strength of God):

God's strength

Romans 1:20,	Psalms 135:6
Ephesians 1:19-20,	2 Corinthians 12:9-10
Revelations 6:15-17	

God's power in the lives of believers

1 Corinthians 2:11-12,	2 Thessalonians 1:11
1 Peter 1:5,	Ephesians 3:16-17
Philippians 3:10,	2 Timothy 4:16-17

God's strength is the believer's comfort

Psalms 27:1, 3,	John 10:28-29
Romans 8:28, 31	

Randy finds Locke's—Walkabout papers

    Disc 1, Episode 4 – Time 19:46-21:45

Michael is injured, Locke presses on

    Disc 1, Episode 4 – Time 22:15-22:38

Locke (in a wheelchair) argues with the agent

    Disc 1, Episode 4 – Time 39:10-40:36

Do you have what it takes?

Episode 5 White Rabbit

Further study on decision making:

Examples of good decision making

Joshua 24:15,   Exodus 18:24-25

Nehemiah 4:21-23,   Matthew 4:19-20

Hebrews 11:25

Examples of bad decision making

Genesis 3:6,   Exodus 32:1-4

Judges 8:23-27,   Hosea 2:5

Mark 14:10-11

Things that should effect our decisions

Psalms 25:4-5,   Psalms 25:8-9

Romans 8:28-30,   Mark 12:29

Hebrews 11:17-19

Jack's dad tells him you don't have what it takes
Disc 2, Episode 5 – Time 10:47-12:35

Locke challenges Jack to take the lead
Disc 2, Episode 5 – Time 27:12-30:38

Charlie's tattoo: Living is easy with eyes closed
Disc 2, Episode 5 – Time 22:44-24:40

Where would you stay?

Episode 6 House of the Rising Son

Further study on putting God first:

Examples of putting God first

Enoch – Genesis 5:22, 23

Noah – Genesis 6:9

Abraham – Genesis 12:4

Hezekiah – 2 Kings 20:3

John the Baptist – John 3:29

Where would you stay?

Examples of not putting God first

Solomon – 1 Kings 11:4

Amaziah – 2 Chronicles 25:2

Judah – Jeremiah 3:10

Exodus 20:3

Motives for compromise

Genesis 26:7

Genesis 16:1

Joshua 7:21

Jack's speech

Disc 2, Episode 5 – Time 37:54-39:51

Decision between beach or cave dwelling

Disc 2, Episode 6 – Time 17:00-18:00

Disc 2, Episode 6 – Time 24:43-26:10

Disc 2, Episode 6 – Time 27:29-28:24

The struggle is nature's way of strengthening it

Episode 7 The Moth

Further study on faith in trials:

Testing of Faith

Revelations 3:10,   2 Peter 2:4-9

2 Thessalonians 1:4,   1 Thessalonians 3:2-4

2 Corinthians 8:1,

Trials

Job 7:17-18,   Psalms 11:5

Isaiah 1:25,   Zechariah 13:9

Malachi 3:3

Examples of God's Testing

Judges 2:20-3:4,   Deuteronomy 8:16

Judges 7:4-7,   Genesis 22:1

2 Corinthians 12:7-9

Charlie gives Locke his drugs

Disc 2, Episode 6 – Time 32:25-34:21

Disc 2, Episode 7 – Time 5:33-6:17

Locke uses moth as an illustration

Disc 2, Episode 7 – Time 19:15-20:34

I became the man
I was hunting

Episode 8 Confidence Man

Further study on the effects of sin:

Effects of sin on the Earth

Genesis 3:17

Leviticus 18:25

Effects of sin on individuals

Isaiah 57:20-21

John 8:34

1 Corinthians 15:56

Effects of sin on the sinner before God

>Isaiah 64:6

>Ezra 9:6

>Isaiah 59:2

Sawyer's vengeance

Disc 2, Episode 8 – Time 9:45-13:08

9

You deserve a break, Today!

Episode 9 Solitary

Sawyer's confession—I became the man I was hunting

Disc 2, Episode 8 – Time 34:50-37:08

Sayid—What I did today... I swore I'd never do again

Disc 2, Episode 8 – Time 40:00-41:10

Further study on stress:

Experiencing stress

- Psalms 38:8

- Mark 14:33-39

Causes of stress

- Deuteronomy 28:65

- 1 Corinthians 7:33

- 2 Corinthians 11:28

- Ecclesiastes 1:13

God comforts those under stress

- Psalms 102:2

- Matthew 11:28

- John 16:33

Sullivan's rash and the doctor's prescription

Disc 3, Episode 9 – Time 4:50-6:08

Kate's comment on Jack smiling

Disc 3, Episode 9 – Time 31:30-32:56

Adoption: A Chosen One

Episode 10 Raised By Another

Further study on adoption:

Adoption in the Bible

- Genesis 15:3

- Exodus 2:10

- Ester 2:7

- Deuteronomy 14:4

Believers are adopted by God

- 1 John 3:1-2

- 2 Corinthians 6:18

- Ephesians 1:5

- Galatians 4:7-9

Adoption benefits and responsibilities

- Proverbs 14:26

Adoption: A Chosen One

- Matthew 6:31-33

- Psalms 94:14

- John 12:35-36

- 2 Corinthians 6:17-18

- 1 Peter 1:14

Claire finds out see is pregnant

Disc 3, Episode 10 – Time 5:53-8:09

Malkin and Clare discuss adoption

Disc 3, Episode 10 – Time 26:55-27:40

Offers Claire money and the plane ticket

Disc 3, Episode 10 – Time 36:20-38:50

Thomas' statement—...best thing ever.

Disc 3, Episode 10 – Time 7:30-7:53

Not on the list

Episode11

All the Best Cowboys Have Daddy Issues

Further study on salvation:

Salvation is necessary

- Isaiah 59:1-2

- Romans 7:14-20

- Ephesians 2:1-5

- Romans 3:28

- 1 Peter 3:18

Things that change once saved

- Philippians 3:20

- Ephesians 2:13

- Romans 5:1-2

- 2 Corinthians 5:17

- 1 John 1:7

Ethan is not on the list

Disc 3, Episode 10 – Time 41:42-42:03

Disc 3, Episode 11 – Time 0:00-1:13

The Key

Episode 12 Whatever the Case May Be

Further study on independence:

Reasons for loneliness

- Isaiah 59:2

- Psalms 142:4

- John 4:9

- Luke 7:12

- Ecclesiastes 4:8

Good from solitude

- Matthew 6:6

- Exodus 3:1-2

- Mark 1:35

- Mark 9:2

Fellowship

- 1 John 4:10

The Key

- Acts 2:42

- Psalms 55:14

- Acts 1:14

- Hebrews 13:16

Sawyer can't pick the lock

Disc 3, Episode 12 – Time 14:52-15:34

Disc 3, Episode 12 – Time 17:04-17:53

Jack and Kate dig up the key

Disc 3, Episode 12 – Time 27:18-29:08

Kate says—I can take care of myself

Disc 3, Episode 12 – Time 2:02-2:20

\Rose talks with Charlie

Disc 3, Episode 20 – Time 38:15-40:00

Time to let go

Episode 13 Hearts and Minds

Further study on commitment:

God desires commitment

- Joshua 24:14

- Deuteronomy 27:10

- Romans 6:17

- Romans 12:1-3

The benefit of commitment

- Proverbs 16:3

- Deuteronomy 7:9

Examples of Commitment

- Genesis 22:17

- Numbers 12:7

- 1 Kings 15:5

- 2 Chronicles 15:17

- Nehemiah 13:14

Boone wants to tell Shannon about the hatch

Disc 4, Episode 13 – Time 12:25-13:48

Locke says—It's time to let go.

Disc 4, Episode 13 – Time 13:50-15:25

Boone chooses to tell Shannon

Disc 4, Episode 13 – Time 34:08-36:00

Locke says—It's time to let go – follow me.

Disc 4, Episode 13 – Time 41:25-42:33

"He seems to hate it" "What?" "Being a dad"

Episode 14 Special

Further study on Fathering:

God as our Father

- 1 Corinthians 8:6

- Hosea 11:1

- Psalms 68:5

- Deuteronomy 8:5

- Matthew 6:9

- John 1:12-13

Responsibilities of Fathers

- Psalms 203:24

- Proverbs 13:24

- Psalms 78:2-8

- Colossians 3:21

Examples of Fathers (Good and Bad)

- Genesis 18:19

- Luke 1:5-20

- Luke 15:11-31

- Genesis 25:28

- 1 Samuel 2:22-25

He seems to hate it—What?—Being a dad.

Disc 4, Episode 14 – Time 0:59-1:44

Walt and mom leave Michael

Disc 4, Episode 14 – Time 6:19-8:42

Michael confesses he doesn't know how to relate to Walt

Disc 4, Episode 14 – Time 8:48-9:46

Walt criticizes Michael for not being there for him

Disc 4, Episode 14 – Time 18:44-19:47

Michael gives Walt all the cards he had sent

Disc 4, Episode 14 – Time 38:44-40:06

Under Attack

Episode 15 Homecoming

Further study on Attacks:

Israel Attacked

- Exodus 17:8-12

- Judges 6:1-6

- 2 Samuel 10:8

- 2 Kings 17:3-6

Attacks on Individuals

- Acts 16:22

- Genesis 4:8

- 1 Samuel 19:9

Protection from Attacks

- Ephesians 6:13-18

- Psalms 18:1-3

- 2 Timothy 4:18

God defends his people

- Isaiah 41:10

- Psalms 34:7

- Isaiah 19:20

- Mathew 16:18

- Isaiah 31:1

- 2 Chronicles 16:7

Ethan attacks Charlie and Jin in the woods

Disc 4, Episode 15 – Time 9:12-11:20

Ethan caught

Disc 4, Episode 15 – Time 32:43-35:25

Charlie shoots Ethan

Disc 4, Episode 15 – Time 35:42-36:16

Claire says she wants to trust Charlie

Disc 4, Episode 15 – Time 39:43-40:53

"I never carried a letter around for twenty years because I couldn't get over my baggage"

Episode 16 Outlaws

Further study on guilt:

God and guilt

- Psalms 69:5

- Genesis 4:8

- 1 Corinthians 4:4-5

- 2 Chronicles 24:18

- Numbers 14:18

Humans and guilt

- Psalms 51:3-5

- Hebrews 9:9

- Leviticus 5:17

- Isaiah 59:1-3

Justification through Jesus

- Romans 5:9

- Romans 8:3-4

- Romans 4:25

- 1 Corinthians 1:30

- Romans 1:17

- Galatians 3:11

Game:—I never ...

Disc 4, Episode 16 – Time 17:59-22:01

Post traumatic stress disorder - Guilt

Disc 4, Episode 16 – Time 15:31-16:08

Disc 4, Episode 16 – Time 33:04-34:52

Sawyer finds out he was tricked

Disc 4, Episode 16 – Time 36:27-37:40

17

— God Knows That

Episode 17 ...In Translation

Further study on God's control:

God knows all

- Matthew 10:30

- Job 34:21

- Matthew 6:8

- Isaiah 46:10

- 1 Chronicles 28:9

God is in control of all

- Luke 1:37

- Job 42:2

- Deuteronomy 4:39

- Revelations 4:11

God is sovereign

- Psalms 93:1

- 1 Chronicles 29:12

- Matthew 10:29-30

- Philippians 1:29

- Psalms 95:3

Sun slaps Michael and later explains

Disc 5, Episode 17 – Time 2:10-3:33

Disc 5, Episode 17 – Time 6:29-7:20

Sun yells in English

Disc 5, Episode 17 – Time 25:50-30:31

Jin pounds the man so he won't be shot

Disc 5, Episode 17 – Time 23:09-24:09

Jin is forgiven and starts over

Disc 5, Episode 17 – Time33:25-36:06

4 8 15 16 23 42 < 1

Episode 18 Numbers

Further study on one God:

God is one

- Deuteronomy 6:4

- 1 Corinthians 8:4

- Galatians 3:20

- Mark 12:29

There is only one God

- Deuteronomy 6:4

- 1 Timothy 2:5

- Mark 12:29

- Ephesians 4:6

One God worthy

- 1 Kings 8:23

- Exodus 20:3-5

- Psalms 81:9

- Mark 12:30

- Isaiah 37:19

Hurley sees the numbers on the papers

    Disc 5, Episode 18 – Time 1:30-2:36

Hurley wins the lottery

    Disc 5, Episode 18 – Time 2:55-3:40

Leonard keeps rattling the numbers

    Disc 5, Episode 18 – Time 18:43-21:24

Danielle agrees the numbers are cursed

    Disc 5, Episode 18 – Time 32:00-36:11

The numbers listed on the hatch

    Disc 5, Episode 18 – Time 42:03-42:24

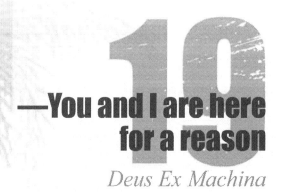

—You and I are here for a reason

Deus Ex Machina

Further study on God and purpose:

The purposes of God will be fulfilled

- Isaiah 46:10-11

- Proverbs 16:4

- Ephesians 1:11

- Psalms 33:11

- Job 42:2

God cannot be stopped

- Proverbs 19:21

- Job 9:12

- Daniel 4:25

- Revelations 17:17

God's Purpose

- Ephesians 3:10-11

- 2 Timothy 1:9

- Exodus 9:16

- Isaiah 29:11

- John 6:40

I want to tell you that you're special, very special. You're part of a design

Disc 5, Episode 19 – Time 6:07-7:22

But you and I are here for a reason.

Disc 5, Episode 19 – Time 23:12-24:56

...like someone steam rolled Harry Potter.

Disc 5, Episode 19 – Time 28:11-30:35

A light in the hatch shines through

Disc 5, Episode 19 – Time 41:18-41:55

A Time to be Born, A Time to Die

Episode 20 Do No Harm

Further study on death:

Death

- Ecclesiastes 12:7

- Romans 5:12

- Psalms 89:48

- Job 14:5

Death of Believers

- Romans 14:8

- Philippians 1:21-23

- Luke 23:43

- 1 Corinthians 15:55

Death of Unbelievers

- Psalms 49:10

- Proverbs 10:27

- John 8:21,24

- Revelations 20:13

- Daniel 12:2

- 2 Kings 20:1

Boone's Death

Disc 5, Episode 20 – Time 34:21-36:08

Disc 5, Episode 20 – Time 37:43-38:54

Claire fights giving birth

Disc 5, Episode 20 – Time 28:31-29:41

The child is born

Disc 5, Episode 20 – Time 36:09-37:42

Celebrating life, grieving death

Disc 5, Episode 20 – Time 38:58-41:32

Episode 21 The Greater Good

Further study on motives:

Examples of bad motives

- Matthew 2:7-13

- Ester 3:1-9

- John 12:4-6

- Titus 1:10-11

Actions and motives

- Philippians 1:15-18

- 1 Samuel 18:20-23

- 1 Kings 8:17-19

- Matthew 1:18-20

Jesus' motives

- John 8:29

- Hebrews 10:5-7

- John 4:34

Sayid's motive in helping CIA

Disc 6, Episode 21 – Time 2:41-4:47

Locke's motive for stopping the signal

Disc 6, Episode 21 – Time 25:26-27:21

Sayid's motive in helping terrorists

Disc 6, Episode 21 – Time 35:23-36:48

"You always want to run away"

Episode 22 Born To Run

Further study on fleeing:

Fleeing

- Exodus 23:27

- Joshua 7:12

- 1 Samuel 19:11-12

- John 10:2-5

Running from something

- John 1:1-10

- 2 Timothy 2:22

- 1 Timothy 6:11

- Jonah

- Psalms 16:4

- Galatians 2:2

- Proverbs 4:10-12

- Philippians 2:14-16

Sawyer knows Kate wants on the raft to run

Disc 6, Episode 22 – Time 10:33-12:00

You always want to run away.

Disc 6, Episode 22 – Time 23:24-25:13

Kate tells why she has to run

Disc 6, Episode 22 – Time 32:48-35:00

23

Message in a Bottle

Episode 23 Exodus Part 1

Further study on the Bible:

Authority of the Bible

- Matthew 22:29

- 2 Timothy 3:14-15

- Acts 7:11

- Psalms 119:89

- Matthew 24:34-36

Purpose of the Bible

- Psalms 19:7-11

- John 20:30

- Romans 15:4

- 1 Kings 17:24

- Psalms 1:1-2

Sufficiency of the Bible

- Deuteronomy 4:1-2

- Hebrews 1:1-2

- Romans 7:12

- Psalms 19:7

Charlie collects messages for the bottle
Disc 6, Episode 23 – Time23:31-24:12
Disc 6, Episode 23 – Time38:50-40:00

Walt – Vincent (dog) is a good listener
Disc 6, Episode 23 – Time 31:03-32:36

Jin – I am in this place because I'm being punished
Disc 6, Episode 23 – Time 36:14-38:20

"Each one of us was brought here for a reason"

Episode 24 Exodus Part 2

Further study on meaning:

Human Race

- Genesis 5:1-2

- Genesis 1:26-28

- Genesis 2:16-17

- Matthew 12:36

- Matthew 4:4

- Ephesians 2:10

- John 14:12

- John 10:10

- Colossians 3:1-3

- Micah 6:8

Sawyer reads the messages in the bottle

Disc 6, Episode 24 – Time 27:55-28:53

Sun asks Shannon if she thinks we are being punished

    Disc 6, Episode 24 – Time 37:48-39:09

Each one of us was brought here for a reason

    Disc 6, Episode 24 – Time 57:14-1:01:00

About the Authors

Dr. Randy T. Johnson has been married to Angela for over 25 years. They have two children, Clint and Stephanie. He has been Chaplain and Bible teacher at Oakland Christian School in Auburn Hills, Michigan for about 20 years. He also ministers at two local Chinese Church youth groups. He wrote And Then Some and created Read316.com.

David Rutledge has been working in youth ministry for over 10 years as a Bible teacher, a youth pastor and a speaker. David has a degree in Biblical Studies/Christian Education of Youth and History from Cedarville University, a Masters of Education from Regent University and is currently finishing up his Doctorate of Education from Liberty University. David lives with his wife Rebekah and children in Burbank California.

To order additional copies of *Lost Lessons* or to find out more by Chaplain Dr. Randy Johnson, David Rutledge or other life changing books published by Zoë Life Publishing, please visit our website www.zoelifepub.com.

Discounts are available for ministry and retail purposes.

Contact Outreach at Zoë Life Publishing

Zoë Life Publishing
P.O. Box 871066
Canton, MI 48187
(877) 841-3400
outreach@zoelifepub.com

Made in the USA
Charleston, SC
25 November 2011